The Supervision of Construction

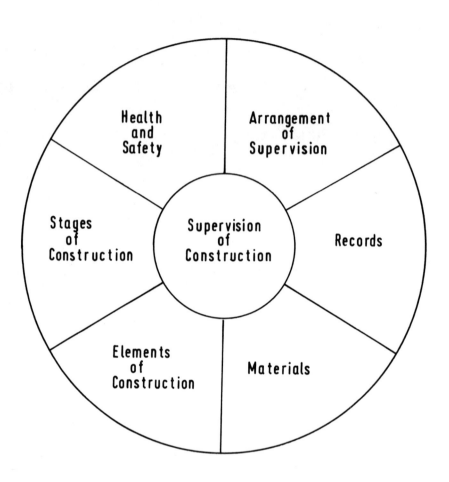

The Supervision of Construction

A guide to site inspection

John W Watts MICE

Batsford Academic and Educational Limited London

First published 1980
ISBN 0 7134 2173 8

Printed in Great Britain by
Redwood Burn Ltd
Trowbridge & Esher
for the publishers
Batsford Academic and Educational Limited
4 Fitzhardinge Street London W1H 0AH

Contents

Acknowledgment

I would like to express my grateful acknowledgements to:

Betty Martin and Betty King for their typing;
G H Watts, my father, for the chapter Structural Steelwork;
My colleagues, especially T G Holden, for their assistance, advice and criticism;
Mr Patrick Kinnersly, for permission to use material from his article Health Hazard Guide which appeared in the 23 November 1978 issue of *New Civil Engineer*;
Newnes-Butterworths, publishers, for permission to use material from *Civil Engineer's Reference Book*;
Thelma M Nye for her kind editorial help and encouragement.

Marlborough 1980   J W W

Introduction

The idea for the book came to me after I had made a return to design office work, having spent several continuous years on site, and was busy relearning design office disciplines. It occurred to me that I might be able to be of use to those undertaking the reverse process — that is to say, making the transition from the theoretical to the practical — by attempting to explain how the standards of design and specification developed in a design office are enforced on site.

This book, then, is written from a Consultant's point of view and is intended to be a guide for those who are new to the business of supervising construction works and who, ideally, possess a technical training. It is thus written primarily for graduates, site bound straight from college or university and for those who have had some design office experience and are about to take up their first site appointment.

Informed supervision is the link between design and construction. Just as good design is difficult to achieve without a knowledge of construction, so good supervision is difficult to achieve without a knowledge of design. Depending on the quality of supervision afforded during construction, the quality of a finished job may range from downright dangerous, through safe (but never really working properly), or satisfactory in all major respects, to fulfilling the requirements of the specification in every respect. Happily most examples of construction fall within the last two descriptions.

The requirements of supervision may be summarised as being:

Regular systematic inspection.
A careful keeping and maintaining of records.
A knowledge of the principles and pattern of design.
A knowledge of the order in which things are done.
A sense of proportion and a great deal of perseverance.

With these points in mind, and with constant vigilance, a well constructed job will result.

The book is arranged in ten chapters. It describes what is important in site supervision and how best to set about it. Each chapter deals with an important aspect of site work and is preceded by a diagram explaining the chapter's contents. Although these aspects are here considered separately, chapter by chapter, they should be applied both separately and as a whole during supervision. Specialised construction techniques, for example, those employed in tunnelling and diving are described briefly, and chapter 8 is devoted to a selec-

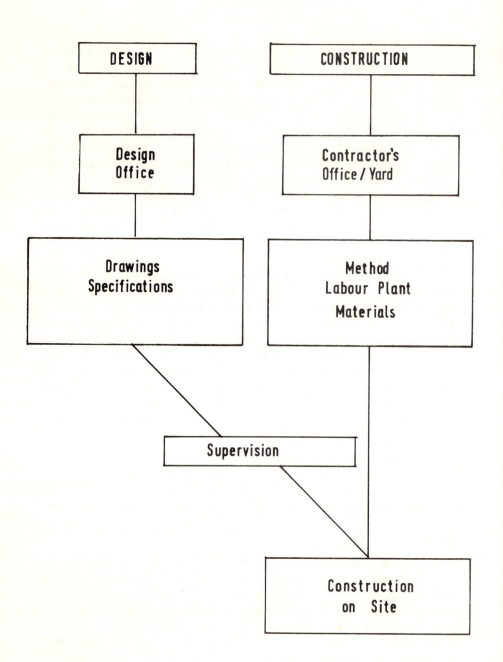

Diagram A

tion of such items, treating each briefly. Electrical and mechanical works are included in so far as their installation affects construction.

Chapter 10, General Observations, contains a summary of the contents of the chapters, an explanation of the diagrams, and some general comments on supervision. This chapter could conveniently be read first in order to obtain a general impression of the procedures described in the separate chapters.

ARRANGEMENT OF SUPERVISION

Resident
Engineer / Architect

| Sections.
Engineers
Inspectors
of Works | Laboratory.
Engineers
Technicians | Clerk of
Works | Laboratory.
Technicians |

SITE

Standards of Construction

Construction Sections

Arrangement of sections
   general / particular
   strength
   shifts

Inspection procedure
   formal / informal
   separate / continuous

Philosophy of control
   strict
   relaxed

Quality of Materials

Laboratory
   Specialist firm
   Specialist investigation

Routine testing / Inspection

Location
   at source
   arrival on site
   made on site

Arrangement
   as required
   independently

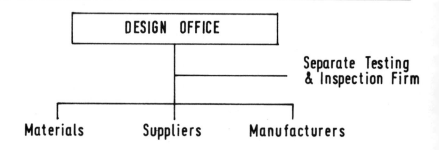

DESIGN OFFICE

Separate Testing
& Inspection Firm

| Materials | Suppliers | Manufacturers |

Diagram 1

14

1 Arrangement of Supervision

Throughout this book the meaning of *supervision of construction* relates to the practical supervision and inspection of construction in the field and does not mean supervision of construction in the sense of project management. The book is written from a consultant's point of view and assumes the conventional Consultant/Contractor/Client relationship common in construction work. It is nevertheless appropriate in any situation where supervised construction is proceeding, for example, works constructed under Direct Labour arrangements or under Turnkey Contracts.

The term *Inspector* means any person of whatever trade, profession or seniority employed in supervising the construction of the works. This single term is used for the sake of simplicity though in the various contexts found in the book it will represent persons more properly called, for example, Engineer, Architect, or Clerk of Works.

The term *Contractor* means the firm undertaking the actual construction of the works.

'*Construction*' means works usually thought of as 'civil engineering' as well as works usually thought of as 'building'.

The word 'should' has been used throughout, even where 'must' would be more appropriate — circumstances and experience will soon differentiate which is the more appropriate word to use.

Construction sites come in all shapes and sizes; extended as for a motorway, compact as for a factory, extensive as for a new town development, small as for a water tower. They also come in a wide range of complexities from the higly specialised content of a nuclear power station to the simple form of a housing development. This is not to imply that only the large sites are complex or the small ones simple. Most sites are a mixture of simple and complex and their relative proportions on any one site frequently change as construction progresses. Whatever the type of project the supervision of its construction is an important matter and the choice of staff and the arrangements of supervision on site need careful consideration. Good practices and standards of workmanship do not automatically accrue from a well-written contract and a tight specification. Positive practical supervision is required to ensure that the desired standards are attained.

An initial careful assessment of the varying requirements of site supervision for a project will have been made at the Inspector's Head Office and the selected required staff consequently directed to the site. Their actual deployment on site will then depend almost entirely on the Contractor's working hours and programme of construction. The strength of the inspecting team will vary during the construction period starting with a few when the site opens, building up as the volume of work increases and, lastly, reducing as construction approaches and then reaches completion. Not only will the numerical strength of the inspecting team vary during the construction period, but also their actual deployment will vary during this period as the various construction activities comprising the project commence, progress and terminate. Obviously all activities do not commence simultaneously on the first day of the contract and reach completion on the last day. Activities build up from zero, peak about halfway through the contract period and then tail off to completion.

Site supervision falls broadly into two main divisions:

1 The supervision of the standards of construction
2 The detailed checking and testing of the materials of construction

The supervision of construction standards is undertaken as an overall site-wide inspection routine proceeding simultaneously with construction. The checking and testing of materials entails the sampling and testing of construction materials at source, on arrival at site and on their incorporation in the permanent work, and is organised from and by the site laboratory. For convenience the workings of these two broad divisions are described separately although in practice they are very closely interrelated.

Site supervision is also a mixture of the general and the particular. That is to say that there are certain activities which will be within the experience of most Inspectors and there are other activities which are more specialised and hence require a specialist knowledge of supervision. The balance between general and particular depends on the type of project or even the particular phases of construction passed through during the progress of a project. Supervision may therefore be arranged *territorially* or *sectionally*. In the *territorial arrangement* each Inspector is responsible for all the activities falling within a certain area, whereas in the *sectional arrangement* each Inspector is assigned responsibility for one or more particular activity wherever that activity may be progressing. It may be seen that the territorial approach is satisfactory where general construction work, such as site clearance excavation, simple foundations and superstructure, are concerned. Where the work becomes more specialised, as for instance with piling, structural steelwork and prestressed concrete, a more specialised knowledge is required and thus the arrangement of supervision by class of work becomes the more appropriate method. In practice, most projects will probably entail a mixture of both systems from time to time as work proceeds. Once established, and allowing for some trial and error, the arrangements for supervision should not be changed without good reason and the separate limits of responsibilities must be clearly defined at all times.

It is not only the type of project which determines supervisory arrangements, but also the manner and means employed by the Contractor in executing the work. These will be determined by the type of project and are often possible to anticipate. All housing developments will have a good deal in common, so will all power station contracts and all dock projects, and so the experiences gained on past projects will be used to anticipate the methods of working and supervisory arrangements necessary for forthcoming works of a similar kind.

Having satisfactorily arranged the supervision to meet the circumstances of the site, the next step is for the Inspector to agree with the Contractor a procedure whereby the Contractor presents for inspection a section of the works and the Inspector inspects it. This is the basic arrangement of inspection procedure though in practice it is not always, and does not need to be, so clear cut. Neither is it always the best approach as explained below.

Under the conditions of a contract the Contractor undertakes to execute the works to the required standards of workmanship and quality of materials as required by the specification. It is with the attainment of these standards that site supervision is concerned and thus it normally becomes necessary to exercise quality control on the Contractor's production rather like the many quality control checks exercised in the production of goods in a factory. The simile cannot be taken much further because whereas in a factory the environment is controlled, most of the work is monotonously repetitive and the factory and its systems are established to operate for perhaps many years developing and improving gradually, each construction project is a one-off event being set up, constructed and completed in a relatively short time. A three year construction phase covers most construction projects, with very large projects taking say five years.

How controls are imposed and operated depends very much on the personalities and preferences of the Inspector and the Contractor. It is essential for the smooth running of a project that the system of control for any given operation is discussed and agreed beforehand by both Inspector and Contractor, the former desiring to ensure that required standards are consistently and uniformly achieved, the latter wishing to execute the works in as economical a way as possible and without hinderance by perhaps seemingly unnecessary control. In the present context, control is taken to mean the various systems and procedures by which the Inspector wishes to inspect and check the quality and standards of work during construction.

Control may be rigid or relaxed, formal or informal, depending

17

entirely on the type of work in question and those responsible for its execution and supervision. It must be emphasised that a rigid formal arrangement does not mean automatically that working relationships are unharmonious. In many circumstances the rigid and formal approach is the only one possible under which both parties can achieve their required aims, and construction progress is achieved smoothly and harmoniously as a result. At the other extreme, a relaxed informal arrangement can lead very easily to misunderstandings and loss of control, again by both parties.

Secondary site offices

On extensive sites it becomes almost essential to establish secondary site offices or section offices remote from the main site office in order to maintain more immediate contact with the work progressing on site. These section offices may be cabins or caravans, semi-portable, wheel or skid mounted, or they may be existing houses which lie within the site area and which have been acquired with the site. The offices should have the basic services of water, lighting and heating, be provided with adequate basic furniture and be weatherproof and secure. Many Inspectors have their own favourite designs for section offices, formed through many years experience, and arrange to have them custom-built if the contract so allows. The section offices can become a useful on-site meeting place, away from the more formal atmosphere and restraints of the main site office, and indeed their main purpose is to function as control centres for the supervision and inspection of the sections they serve.

It is most important to ensure that each Inspector has his own base, be it a desk in a shared office or a separate cabin on site, where he can study the drawings, maintain records, write his diary, discuss items with the Contractor, receive and deal with requests for inspection, and carry out all the other day-to-day tasks required in site supervision. Section offices should be provided with all the drawings relevant to each particular section and be kept up to date with revisions as they are issued. Copies of the specifications and bills of quantities should also be kept at section office, photocopies of the relevant portions if bound copies are not available, and diaries, record proforma, bending schedules and all other items utilised in inspecting directing and recording the daily progress of the works.

Transport

Transport for the Inspector, if provided under the terms of the contract as is usually the case in overseas projects, is usually a matter of ceaseless wrangles because this never appears to be sufficient. Transport always seems to be in for routine service, under repair or despatched on priority errands. It is a state of affairs that has to be accepted and made the best of.

Working hours

Because supervision should be exercised whenever and wherever permanent work is in progress, the Contractor's working hours have a direct influence on the strength of the supervisory staff required and their own working hours.

The general run of construction projects probably operate to a single shift daytime hours timetable, commencing at say 8 am and finishing at 6 pm though the finishing time does depend to some extent on the time of year. Generally speaking though much the same hours are worked summer and winter, with site lighting being provided during winter. It is a fallacy to imagine that winter hours will be much less than summer hours.

If the construction programme demands it, a two shift system may be introduced extending the working day from say 6 am to 10 pm. Such a system may be considered necessary to take advantage of daylight hours or to avoid excessive daytime temperatures during part of the year, or it may be a permanent arrangement for the construction period.

A working day of twenty-four hours is not particularly common except perhaps in very large and complex projects, and in certain specialised forms of construction such as tunnelling, slide work and tide work because the arrangement requires a large labour force and a similarly enhanced supervisory team. Twenty-four hour working is usually covered on a three-by-eight hour shift basis, say 6 am to 2 pm, 2 pm to 10 pm and 10 pm to 6 am though occasionally on a short term basis only, a two by twelve hour shift arrangement may be more suitable or convenient. It is a desirable practice to undertake all the careful preparatory work during daylight hours, leaving the routine straightforward activities for the night shift.

As soon as more than one shift is worked, many additional factors come into the arrangement of supervision, three shifts naturally requiring more accompanying facilities than two, and the Contractor is obliged to give adequate notice to the Inspector when he intends to introduce shift work. For a start, more inspecting staff are required and they may require extra transport, office accommodation, meals, lighting, record proforma, sets of drawings and other documents. When arranging shift hours a short hand-over period between shifts should be allowed for. Co-ordination between those on shift duty and senior staff who are working routine hours becomes more difficult, but is vital and should be maintained. It requires good record keeping and regular briefing and de-briefing sessions. Senior staff should also make a point of visiting the site fairly regularly, over and above their normal day, when shift work is in progress.

Such visits are often a mixture of supervision and morale boosting and, if things are going well, they should be kept brief. Personnel to be contacted in times of difficulties or emergencies must be designated and their addresses and telephone numbers noted. Special arrangements with or notification to the local emergency services ie police, fire, ambulance, may be advisable, and so too are arrangements with gate keepers if the work is being undertaken on an existing works site, for instance, on an extension to a power station or factory.

A check should also be made that the Contractor really has made adequate provisions of his own for labour, supervisory staff, breakdown repairs and so on. If a machine breaks down it is usually at night, with no mechanic available to repair it, and a shift's output might consequently be lost.

It is customary to allow breaks or days-off for staff engaged on shift work duties, and replacements should be arranged during these periods. Staff on shift duty usually prefer to work the same shift for long periods rather than alternating between shifts because of the period of adjustment they require when changing shift. From the point of view of continuity in supervision, it is also advantageous to keep the frequency of changes in personnel on any one shift as low as possible. The time necessary to switch one person from day shift to night shift (or vice versa) and work in his replacement is usually spread over three days allowing a twenty-four hour break between successive shifts for each person concerned. It is a procedure which cannot be accomplished overnight.

When preparing a chart or rota for supervisory duties, due allowance should be made for the holiday periods which occur under various names and in various lengths in different countries. Weekends, annual leave, home leave, local leave, religious holidays, public holidays and national holidays are examples of such occasions which may play havoc with duty rotas unless they are anticipated. Staff levels should be arranged to cater for these circumstances. Staff absence through sickness or other reasons, must also be covered as and when it occurs. It is all too easy under such circumstances to provide, in the first instance, makeshift arrangements which, as time passes, become established as permanent. It is when routine is overlooked or forsaken for the sake of expediency that the quality of supervision is reduced without its becoming apparent until perhaps things start going wrong.

Lastly, another item to arrange is the relief of inspecting staff engaged on the supervision of long continuous activities such as massive concrete pours. A relief for meals and cups of tea at appropriate times is a small but very important point too often overlooked.

The two broad divisions of inspection defined earlier in this chapter will now be considered further.

1   The supervision of the standards of construction

A formal system will usually entail the Contractor applying with due notice for inspection of a particular item of work by means of specially printed forms or 'check-out' cards on which are listed the several items involved in the construction. In concrete work these could be blinding, class of concrete, shutters, cover, reinforcement, built-in items and water bar, with a box against each to be marked as requiring inspection. After inspection, the boxes will be marked by the Inspector as being either satisfactory or requiring further attention, final approval being given only when all items are satisfactory. At the time of approval, notice should also be passed to the site laboratory where appropriate. This system is repeated for each individual element of construction until the works are complete. The cards in themselves form a detailed record of every single operation and should be stored safely in case the need of future reference arises, as it usually does. In complex constructions involving services and built-in items as for a power house, or say as in a concrete dam, each single pour will be preplanned and individual check-out cards prepared for each pour. These cards will define precisely the pour and will detail all items for inclusion, being virtually drawings in their own right. A similar but less formalised method is the use of hand written requests, usually in duplicate books, presented to the Inspector for his attention.

The simple verbal request for inspection and ensuing verbal approval after inspection, is a satisfactory method for simple straightforward items or where there is a large degree of repetitiveness, simple paving or precast work for instance. Even though request and approval is verbal, the Inspector should nevertheless record the action in his diary or in the site log. The important point in whatever system of control is adopted is that it should be comprehensive. The procedure of approval sought, inspection made, and approval given should be applied to each and every element of the works in question and not just followed in a sporadic fashion.

It is a commonly held opinion, and the technique is widely practised, that control should be exercised rigorously to start with and then relaxed somewhat if the necessary standards are seen to be achieved consistently, whilst still maintaining sufficient grip to ensure that the required standards are maintained. There is no doubt that this approach is a common one and many specifications are written containing these sentiments, ie stringent quality control testing to begin with but relaxing if successive tests show the quality to be satisfactory and uniform.

A different approach is to wait and see what standards are produced in the first instance without stringent control, control being kept in the background, so to speak, rather than in the foreground. Only if repeated attempts at achieving the required quality are unsuccessful, is control tightened in a move designed to bring about the desired improvements. Like the former approach, this one may or may not be appropriate and the optimum system may involve a compromise between the two or even a different approach altogether. It is true that hard uncompromising control can achieve excellent results but, conversely, it can also become a major obstacle in achieving improvements if initially the Contractor is having genuine difficulties in meeting the requirements of the specification. Control should be tempered with common sense.

Some construction operations do not lend themselves readily to division into units for separate inspection, rather the operations are continuous and the need for inspection is consequently continuous also. In these cases the Inspector keeps an everyday watch on operations, calling for corrections and improvements as and when required. Examples of such operations are brickwork construction and structural steelwork erection.

2   The testing of materials

This proceeds concurrently with the inspection of construction. On all but the smallest contracts, laboratory facilities are established on the site to enable materials testing to be carried out conveniently and apace with the demands of construction. Materials testing may be divided into three categories:

    (a)   the inspection and testing of materials in their natural state, or at their place of manufacture;

    (b)   similar procedures for materials delivered to site
        and

    (c)   the testing of materials which are produced on the site itself.

Category (a) includes activities such as visits of inspection to quarries, cement works, brickworks, timber yards and bituminous materials batching plants. Included in category (b) are such as the inspection and testing of stored cement, aggregate stockpiles, bought in precast units and most of the materials held in the Contractor's yard or store. Category (c) entails the heaviest involvement of laboratory time, encompassing the testing of such extensive activities as all site-mixed concrete, bituminous products, paving and earthworks materials and compaction.

Just what arrangements and procedures are made for covering these multitudinous duties depends very much on the available facilities and the personal preferences of those responsible for their operation. Generally speaking there are two methods of approach.

Independent

In the first approach the laboratory is instructed to carry out its duties as though it were an independent testing organisation virtually performing the role of checking on the Inspectors themselves. Under this arragnement the functions of inspection and testing should be closely co-ordinated with the immediate requirements of construction control apart from any other testing programmes being followed — cubes should be made from current concrete pours, compaction and density tests should follow the day-to-day earthworks procedure and progress.

As directed

In the second method the laboratory takes tests andmakes inspections only when called upon to do so by the various sections of the Inspector's site control organisation. In this second approach it might appear that the Laboratory plays a more subservient role than in the first, but this is not the case in practice. It should be recognised that whichever approach is adopted, the role of the laboratory is that of a service department providing data on quality standards to the other site control sections and that close co-ordination between the sections and the site laboratory is essential for efficient, effective control. As with the control of the standards of construction, in laboratory testing the frequency of tests may be high initially until satisfactory standards are being consistently achieved, after which the rate may be reduced to a level which still ensures that satisfactory control is maintained. The rate of testing is usually written into the specification and is linked with the rate of construction, eg so many tests required per given volume of concrete, area of pavement or per shift.

It should now be emphasised that the laboratory section in any site supervision organisation is a most important section and should be capable of operating in its own right. That is to say that it should be suitably staffed, provided with its own transport, brought into discussion on site supervision policy and so on. Apart from its involvement in day to day control, the laboratory may also perform a role akin to a site Research and Development department, undertaking investigations of one-off problems, making spot-checks on selected items which do not require regular inspection or checks on an unusual aspect of an otherwise routine operation. With the continuing development of modern materials and material testing techniques the role and scope of the site laboratory is becoming increasingly important.

On small projects where it may be uneconomical to establish a site laboratory, samples may be taken to an outside independent laboratory for testing and/or analysis. Universities, technical colleges, government institutions and commercial material testing firms can all provide such facilities for sites. These organisations may also be employed when the testing or analysis required is of a nature too specialised to be undertaken in a site laboratory.

23

The foregoing remarks relate particularly to those inspection arrangements which are related and organised directly from the site laboratory, and employing the Inspector's site personnel. There are, however, certain inspection operations which are more conveniently undertaken by specialist materials testing firms retained for the purpose. Particular examples of these operations are the inspection and monitoring at the place of manufacture or assembly of the preparation and fabrication of structural steelwork, and the manufacture and testing of many items of mechanical and electrical plant where these examples form a substantial element of a project or require constant specialist supervision. The retained inspecting firm will be required to submit to the Inspector at site, or Head Office, regular reports on its findings during its works' inspection visits, witness and report on tests and ensure that all required test certificates are forthcoming whether they be from the manufacturer, fromthemselves or from any other organisation. These reports often contain remarks regarding items requiring attention which is best provided on site rather than in the works. Such remarks should be noted for action when the piece in question arrives on site.

2 Records

The subject of the keeping of records should be approached as a positive, immediate means of controlling and monitoring all aspects of construction and it should have as much importance attached to it as is automatically afforded to the regular, on the job supervision of site activities. Each person engaged on supervisory duties should keep careful records of the daily works' activities for which he has responsibility and no construction or other site activity, whether for temporary or permanent works, should proceed unsupervised or unrecorded. This is perhaps rather a council for perfection, but it reflects the attitude which should be adopted towards the keeping of site records.

The term *records* includes, for example, works' diaries, daily reports, laboratory test results, photographs, progress drawings and charts, in fact any facility which is used to record the events, progress and standards of site construction.

To some the keeping of records is a chore, to be done only after constant pestering by seniors, whilst to others it is an interesting and obviously valuable part of site duites. However it may be viewed, the keeping of site records is a vital and major part of the Inspector's supervisory responsibilities and some thought should be given to the way the records are organised in order that duplication and omission of information is avoided. Records are important and should not just be allowed to happen or accumulate haphazardly. Direction is required to ensure that at least all important, pertinent facts are recorded and not omitted or overlooked through lack of experience or supervision. It is a routine which can too easily proceed unmonitored, with deficiencies being brought to light only when, say, defective work is found on site and the records consulted. Some duplication of information perhaps is unavoidable, though this should be in subject matter rather in detail, but it can be minimised by a clear definition of responsibilities between the Inspectors.

The keeping of site records is necessary for two main reasons of equal importance though opposite in character. Firstly records are kept, rather obviously, for reference purposes. It must not be thought though that the need to make reference to records arises perhaps only some time after the project is complete. Almost from the first day on site the need to refer to what has gone before will arise time and time again. Records must therefore be kept up to date, not left uncompleted for weeks before a forlorn attempt is made to complete them retrospectively. The need to reply to a

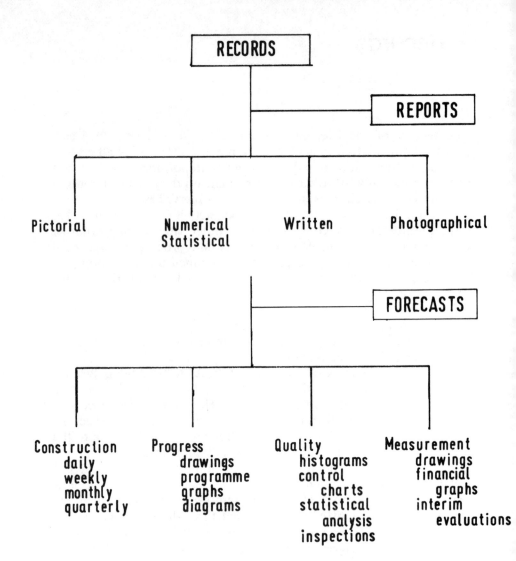

Diagram 2

Contractor's letter or to a question from Head Office will very quickly illustrate the importance of having the correct information to hand promptly.

The second reason for keeping records is that certain forms of record provide a vital, and often the only, tool in the business of monitoring, controlling and predicting the quality and progress of the works. Concrete cube strengths, for example, when suitably presented, will show not only whether the required standards are presently being met but also whether they are likely to be met in the future. If the desired strengths are consistently being exceeded, it may be considered possible to reduce the proportions of cement in the mix, thus affording a saving to the Contractor. If strengths are consistently low, or are showing a tendency to fall, an enhanced mix may be needed. To take another example, record measurements of the volume of earthworks completed over a given period will assist in predicting the rate of similar work in the future. This will be particularly relevant in estimating if work is on schedule or if it needs to be stepped up in order to meet the programme dates.

Although it is part of the responsibility of each Inspector to maintain his own particular records, record keeping is rarely an Inspector's only responsibility and it should never be viewed as an end in itself. There is, on site, perhaps an unfortunate but unavoidable tendency to consider a site man to be doing his job only when he is actually out on site rather than when he is at his desk. How much time an Inspector spends on site and how much time he spends in the office depends, of course, on the job he has to do; a 'field' inspector's place being primarily on site whereas senior staff will be more office bound. Where an Inspector's job is primarily that of supervising work in progress then that must be his first priority with the writing of his records second, but a close second. Good supervision is not affected by Inspectors sitting at their desks most of the day writing reports.

Records are maintained in many ways, but these ways may be broadly grouped into four main categories namely:
1 Written
2 Pictorial
3 Numerical
4 Photographic.
Added to these should be a fifth heading:
5 Reports.

A report is essentially a summary of information on record and report writing an integral part of site records and the main means of conveying information on all site matters to Head Office, clients and other parties. These five headings will now each be considered in turn.

27

1 Written records

These form the largest and most common type of record. It would be impossible to list all the different varieties falling in this category, but some of the most common are described below.

Each Inspector should keep a daily *works' diary* in which should be recorded the significant happenings of the day. It is acknowledged that, as with any diary keeping, some individuals are more conscientious about this than others. At one extreme nothing much may be noted except perhaps appointments, times of meetings and staff leave dates. At the other extreme, the diary becomes a comprehensive log of an individual's or perhaps a section's daily activities, inspections, approvals or rejection of work, meetings, telephone conversations, etc. Whatever the scale, the diary needs to be legible if it is to be of any future value, and the same remark applies to all records. Works' diaries, as distinct from personal diaries, should belong to the project to which they refer, and should be retained with the other project records.

The next item, *daily reports*, is more appropriately discussed here than in the later section on Reports. Daily reports are complementary to, and sometimes serve the purpose of, diaries. The reports discussed in the section on pages 34 to 36 are the more lengthy productions prepared regularly or specially for the purpose of keeping parties, such as Head Office or the Client, informed of general or particular site matters. Daily reports will invariably be required from the Inspectors whose duty it is to supervise the actual construction on site. These reports are conveniently written in duplicate books so that one copy can be handed in to the site office and the other retained by the Inspector. The reports should not be long and should be submitted punctually otherwise the combination of length and lateness will result in the reports not being read in time to be useful. Senior staff normally have to read daily reports from more than one source. The reports should always include details of the work covered, the weather, the number of Contractor's men employed on the section, any delays suffered and their cause, the number and type of plant used and the working hours. A particular note should be kept of the dates on which land is first entered, work started, work completed and the site or portion of the site vacated. Daily reports form the most detailed record of the day-to-day progress of construction on the site and it cannot be over emphasised that they should be written conscientiously and checked frequently to see that they are up to date and contain the required information. It is no good at all leaving the daily reports to accumulate for weeks and then to discover that they are incomplete and their record valueless.

When dealt with, the reports should be filed and stored neatly and chronologically for easy reference. The files should be marked so that they are easily identified say by number, the dates covered and name of author.

As part of normal office procedure, and this is common practice in offices anywhere, a record should be kept of all incoming and outgoing correspondence. Letters, telexes, drawings and other documents should be recorded as they are received or despatched and all copies of all documents received should be date-stamped, not just the top copy.

The practices and procedures which are followed in any well-run 'permanent' office should be established as soon as possible in site offices too. Just because an office is on site, and therefore of a temporary nature, does not mean that office procedures should be loose, in fact because of the generally short life of site offices, the sooner good office procedures are established the better. Procedures should, however, be appropriate to the number of staff available to implement them.

Verbal instructions to the Contractor should always be confirmed in writing and so should telephone conversations where these convey instructions or important information. Written confirmation may, in the first instance, be by hand-written duplicate notes, but it may also require formal correspondence if the subject is of sufficient importance. Copies of all correspondence should be kept whether the correspondence is by means of formal letters or hand-written notes.

Old diaries, note books, field books, etc, should be retained for possible future reference. Initially these are usually kept by their individual owners for their own immediate reference but eventually they should be collected for the central site records as the job nears completion.

The Contractor's labour and plant returns are another common form of written record. These are lists which the Contractor is obliged to submit regularly, usually monthly, giving the number, categories, and type of his labour and plant on site. This information should be checked occasionally though this is easier said than done. On large sites especially, labour is scattered over the site, offices, stores and workshops, split into shifts, off sick or on leave. Plant is also scattered, on haul runs or in the workshops, but at least the larger items are fairly easily accounted for.

The forms, notes, cards or whatever system is employed in the procedure of notifying, inspecting and approving items for construction do in themselves form a most important and comprehensive record of the work when completed. They should therefore be sorted, stored safely and not discarded once the work is finished because they will contain information on virtually each and every element into which the works were broken down for construction. On a large project it will be appreciated that the number of elements can run into thousands when all aspects of construction are considered.

2 Pictorial records

Drawings are a popular and common means of recording information because they are convenient to use, easy to follow and in many cases the best method of representing in the office the progress of construction on the site. The information usually recorded is the date of construction, extent of construction (length, breadth, height) the results of any tests (density, compaction, pressure, etc) and date of approval. In compiling record drawings the approach is one of working from the job back to the drawings as compared to working from the drawings to the job in construction, the former following the latter as work proceeds. Record drawings are thus extremely useful for measuring the progress of construction for evaluation purposes. As well as being used to record information, drawings are also a convenient means of displaying or conveying information, but whatever their use they will quickly lose significance if they are not kept up to date at the intervals appropriate to their function. A drawing intended to record the number of pre-cast units prepared daily is of little value if it is only up-dated weekly.

Record drawings may be purpose-drawn or may be construction drawings suitably amended to record construction progress. Preparing special drawings for record purposes is a good way of assimilating the job in question, but the preparation does take time and it is often more convenient to use an existing drawing, marking it up as necessary. A disadvantage here, maybe, is that the information may only be recorded on a print and thus not easily reproduced if other copies are required. This point is always worth remembering because many reports include progress or record drawings of one kind or another and if these drawings cannot be easily reproduced a good deal of time may be spent in making hand copies. The size and scale of available drawings are also points to be considered. Similarly the marking of progress on such drawings is better done in hatching and symbols rather than in different colours because colour reproduction is rarely available for site prepared reports.

In practice, each site section will probably find it convenient to prepare some drawing or graph on which to record the progress and results appropriate to its particular requirements. These drawings need not be works of art, better that they should be simply drawn, clear and with plenty of room in which to mark up the relevant information. In 'linear' or 'area' construction, eg earthworks or pavements, large sheets of graph paper may be marked to indicate the outlines of the work as divided into the agreed working sections, with these blocked in as constructed and with the results of tests for density, compaction, approval or rejection, levels and so on, successively plotted as the work proceeds. Activities such as services reticulation, pipeline construction, transmission line erection, etc, lend themselves easily to marking up on record drawings. Other activities such as the erection of precast units or structural steelwork, seemingly easily recorded, may in fact prove difficult because of the large number of small units which are frequently involved.

The details shown on the construction drawings frequently require amendment as the work proceeds and these amendments should be marked on the appropriate drawings. Ideally the amendments should be marked directly onto the negative and a revised drawing then issued. Some prints acquire so much additional marked-up information that it is wise to label the prints clearly as record prints and to see that they are safely filed. It is always advisable to keep one print of every revision to each particular drawing so that a complete record of its amendments is available.

To save issuing whole new drawings when only parts are revised 'overlays' are sometimes issued. These should be clearly referenced to the particular drawing to which they refer and the original drawing should also be suitably referenced to its overlay. Another, more common, method is to issue site sketches of the revised area and again these sketches must be referenced to the original drawing and vice versa. These sketches may be specially prepared drawings or may be photocopied from the original drawing with the revisions written in. If revised issues of the original drawing are made, they should be checked to see if all previous amendments have been incorporated. The transference of amendments from old to new prints or the checking that this has been done with the issue of the revised print is a tedious business and a common source of dispute. All separate drawings and sketches, whether intended to revise existing detail or prepared as drawings in their own right, should be dated and numbered, however simply, so that reference may be made to them.

It is especially important that all drawings recording the state of the site before any construction started, and all site general layout drawings, be retained and marked as being record drawings. The importance of carrying out an early survey of the site is explained in chapter 5, Stages of Construction.

In the measurement and recording of quantities, graphs are commonly drawn showing quantities or monetary evaluations plotted against time. These graphs, when compared with the previously estimated progress graphs of the contract, are useful in showing whether the present construction or rate of construction is sufficient to keep the contract running to programme. The contract programme, in bar chart or network form, is a good background on which to mark significant actual construction progress dates. These dates

31

will be recorded in diaries and reports, but it is also useful to have them displayed in relation to the programme as a whole. In this respect the critical path network is particularly appropriate for marking up dates achieved and events of significance to the particular sections involved. Bar charts are especially useful for comparing progress against programme though there is seldom enough room available on the programmes to mark in all the information required. Bar charts are also useful techniques for planning shift work rotas, arranging leaves and general site supervisory duties.

Laboratory statistical data, discussed more fully in the following section, lends itself especially to presentation on control charts, histrograms and other forms of graphical analysis. When the successive results of particular tests are plotted on a chart on which the specification limits are marked, any trends and variations in their values will become apparent far more obviously than if the results were compared numerically. Such graphs are kept by most section offices for their own information as well as being kept by the laboratory.

3 Numerical records

The two sections of a site organisation which probably have the most dealing with numbers and numerical records are the laboratory and the measurement section, the former in its testing and evaluating of site materials and the latter in its measurement of quantities and evaluation of the work done on site.

In its function of sampling, testing, evaluating and recording all the many materials and items of construction which are involved in the routine day-to-day operations on site, the laboratory deals with a very large amount of numerical data and this data has to be systematically assembled, analysed and turned into something useful. Concrete cube strengths, earthworks density, compaction and moisture content determinations, and all the tests involved in the analyses of bituminous product construction are just some examples of the routine daily tests with which the laboratory has to deal.

The data is usually recorded and calculated on standard purpose-designed forms and the results of any series presented to the section offices concerned. Sometimes the information is more usefully presented pictorially by means of graphs, standard sieve analyses being a common example. Statistical analysis of the data usually includes the determination of such parameters as the range, standard deviation and coefficient of variation.

With any routine data the essential point to remember is that in itself it is of not much practical value except as a record-keeping exercise. The data should be assembled and presented in a fashion suitable to enable it to be applied practically, whether this be in numerical or graphical form. It will be the responsibility of the appropriate section office to take whatever action may be considered necessary as a result of the data presented to it. The data will show whether the required standards are being consistently attained, if improvements in production or construction standards are necessary and they will assit in predicting what may be expected in the quality of future work.

There is always ample scope for statistical analyses and these are to be encouraged, provided they are kept within reason. The point to remember is that their presentation should be kept continuously up to date so that trends can be discerned early and any necessary action promptly taken. It is a waste of time and effort if carefully and quickly prepared reports are put aside for study when there is time. Construction is a continuous process where samples should be taken, test results presented, and trends noted and acted on promptly if effective quality control is to be achieved.

The recording of rainfall, temperatures, wind speed, tides, etc, is also usually undertaken by the laboratory.

The measurement of the work done on site is necessary not only to compare progress with programme, but also to evaluate the volume of work for payment to the Contractor. The intervals between payments depends on the size of the project and on the terms of the contract but a usual arrangement is to make payment at monthly intervals.

In the evaluation of the work done, much use is made of record drawings so that the work is measured off these drawings and not physically on site. Occasional physical measurements may be necessary for items such as drainage or cable runs, though as a rule these are measured off the drawings for interim payment purposes. Estimates of the quantities of materials on site will have to be made by direct measurement and observation, these quantities can be considerable and of high value.

In assessing the amount of work completed for interim measurement purposes, it is convenient if standard or average cross sections or volumes can be agreed so that measurement is simplified. This technique saves a great deal of time when assessing the volume of earthworks constructed, concrete poured, aprons filled, etc. Calculating the final volume closely and allowing a percentage of that figure for each evaluation is another means of simplifying interim measurement calculations which can otherwise become tedious and time consuming. Whatever method is employed, care should be taken to ensure that the approximate evaluations do not exceed the value of the accurate final figure. Graphs comparing the actual progress of the works against the programmed requirements for the major items of production in quantity and in monetary terms are usually prepared in whatever detail or breakdown required.

Other records required and maintained by the measurement section are those of labour, (type, hours and rate), plant (ditto) and materials (type and rate) so that estimates of the cost of new or varied work at current or contract rates (if the two differ) can be made or checks made on the value of any claims or estimates submitted by the Contractor. The verification of items executed on daywork rates is a particular case in point. The measurement section will also deal with the other usual items associated with costs and accounts for a site office.

4　Photographic records

The value of having a photographic record of the progress of construction is so obvious that little need be said here except for a few general comments.

Photographic records fall into two categories, the general and the particular. General site photographs are taken on a routine basis usually once a month, and are intended to record general site progress throughout the job. These series often include shots taken from the same location each successive month so that comparisons of progress can be readily made. Site panoramas are another common feature of this type of record.

Particular photographs are made of matters where perhaps difficulties have occurred, as in soil mechanics problems with bank slippage or where the subject matter is of special interest, say in architectural or mechanical details.

With both types of record, a good camera is essential in order to obtain a high standard of detail resolution. It is often the detail discernible in a general photograph which proves the most informative. Ideally two cameras should be available, one for the routine procedures and a second capable of producing instant prints for immediate study. Colour photographs are preferable to black and white though are not always necessary or available to a satisfactory standard.

As with other records, photographs should be identified and kept orderly and safely, ideally by mounting and titling. Similarly, all negatives should be referenced to their prints, recorded and filed.

5　Reports

During the course of a project many reports will be required. The majority of these will be routine progress and technical reports, but a few will be special reports required for subjects demanding particular attention.

Progress reports are usually prepared on a weekly and monthly basis for sending to Head Office with the Client normally receiving a copy of the monthly report. These reports will contain, to an agreed level of detail, information on the period's activities and progress on site, weekly reports being more detailed than those prepared monthly. Progress drawings and graphs are often included with the reports. The information conveyed will be a summary of the week's records on such major items as progress on civil and building construction, mechanical and electrical plant installation, laboratory testing, contractual matters, programme and measurement, staff movements, Contractor's labour force, working hours, etc. Such is the diversity of many large projects that it is common for each section to produce its own section report for inclusion in the whole. Comment is usually kept to a minimum, the individual matters being dealt with under routine correspondence.

Routine technical reports may be desired on specified subjects, for instance on the laboratory testing of concrete, earthworks or bituminous construction. These reports list the period's testing results and are accompanied by the appropriate graphs and statistical analyses. Routine reports may also be required on financial matters though it is often convenient to combine these with the interim contract evaluation for payment of the Contractor.

Once the format and content are established, the preparation of routine reports becomes more or less automatic, though they are nevertheless usually considered a chore by those responsible for their preparation.

The content and emphasis of the routine reports will reflect the stage that construction has reached, characteristically short at start and finish of the contract but longer during the middle stages.

It should be remembered that, particularly with overseas projects, routine reports are the major, and sometimes only, means by which Head Office is kept informed of the progress of construction on site. This point is not always appreciated by site staff who, seeing and supervising the site every day, may not realise the significance of certain events as viewed by Head Office. A lack of information on site progress will place Head Office in a vulnerable position when asked about progress by the Client.

Special reports may be called for on any subject during the construction of the works though they are usually confined to matters of difficulty or of special interest or relevance and in that respect some anticipation is possible. Depending on the subject the report may be brief or lengthy, comprising of just a page or two of typing or it may be a bulky document enclosing appendices of graphs, purpose-made drawings and photographs, and needing many copies. The preparation of such reports is usually far more interesting than the preparation of routine reports but it may involve a considerable amount of time spent searching through the files and records.

At the end of the job a final construction report will be compiled which will encompass all aspects of construction, requiring reference to all site records from start to finish of the project.

It will be seen from this chapter that the keeping of records is not a dull book-keeping job, but an activity that is important in monitoring and controlling the quality and progress of the works.

3 Materials

Although on first appearances all building sites would appear to utilise the same basic construction ingredients of concrete, steelwork and brickwork, and indeed this is very much the case, a better knowledge of the materials will make it clear that although materials of the same family may look the same and be basically the same, they will most likely be very different in their specification. What grade of concrete, what type of cement or class of aggregate? The steelwork could be mild steel or high tensile steel, the brickwork of engineering bricks or facing bricks.

If concrete and steelwork could be termed 'engineering' materials, there are many other materials which may, for the sake of comparison, be termed 'building' materials, eg stone, brick, mortar, plaster, lime, timber, building boards and planks of various compositions. Then there are the 'architectural' materials and finishes, eg paints, glass, tiles, plastics, cladding and panels fabrics. The list is endless and the greater the building element, as opposed to the engineering element of the construction, the greater will be the variety of materials encountered. The point to remember, whatever the project, is that most materials are manufactured or prepared to a specification. The specification could be a British Standard or other international specification, an engineer's or architect's specification or a manufacturer's specification. The specification will have been drafted on a combination of laboratory testing and practical experience and the site laboratory will find itself very heavily involved in the sampling and testing of materials, raw and manufactured. In fact, so varied is the range of present-day construction materials that the testing of many of them, which could require a specialist knowledge of metallurgy, chemistry or geology, for example, is beyond the practical scope of a conventional site laboratory, in which case a firm specialising in materials testing is employed. If the scope demands, the testing firm may establish its own laboratory on site or samples for testing may be despatched to the firm's main laboratory. Government establishments, universities and technical colleges are also examples of establishments which maintain laboratories which may accept samples for testing. The study of materials and their specifications is an absorbing subject in itself, outside the scope of this chapter where only the more commonly used construction materials are described. Even the most commonplace material can cause trouble if not monitored and the purpose of this chapter is to consider the more commonly used construction materials, the

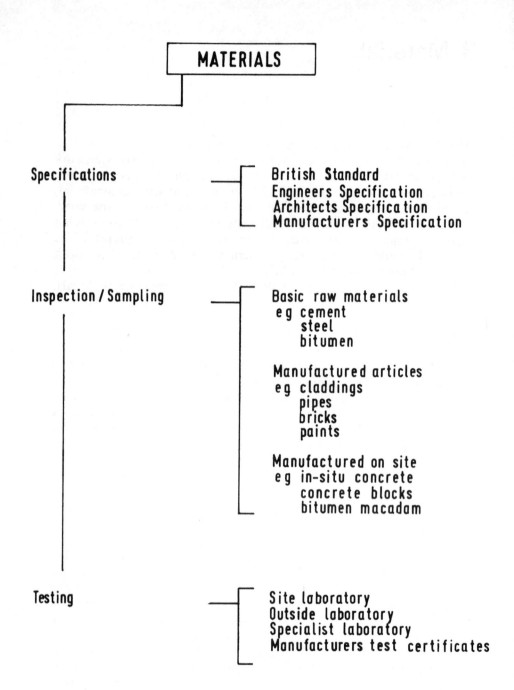

MATERIALS

Specifications
- British Standard
- Engineers Specification
- Architects Specification
- Manufacturers Specification

Inspection / Sampling
- Basic raw materials
  - e g cement
  - steel
  - bitumen
- Manufactured articles
  - e g claddings
  - pipes
  - bricks
  - paints
- Manufactured on site
  - e g in-situ concrete
  - concrete blocks
  - bitumen macadam

Testing
- Site laboratory
- Outside laboratory
- Specialist laboratory
- Manufacturers test certificates

Diagram 3

importance of identifying and separating the various grades of similar items and their reception and storage on site. The materials concerned are a selection of raw and manufactured items some of which will be processed on site to form further materials and other materials which will be used in the form they are received. Examples of the former are sands, aggregates and cement to make concrete or bitumen, sand fillers and aggregates to make asphalt or bituminous macadam. Examples of the latter are structural steelwork and factory made precase concrete units. The materials considered here are:

Blacktop
Bricks (clay)
Cement
Concrete blocks
Lime and plaster
Pipes
Sands and aggregates
Steel reinforcement for concrete
Structural steelwork
Timber

Also included are the following site facilities associated with materials:

Batching plants
Contractor's stores
The laboratory
Quarry and crushing plant

Blacktop

The word 'blacktop' is a convenient and descriptive term commonly used to refer to the many bituminous mixtures employed in road and pavement construction but usually understood to mean structural pavements as opposed to surface dressing.

The most widely used materials in bituminous construction are tar macadam, bitumen macadam and asphalt. The first two are mixtures of graded coated stone, essentially open textured, though dense varieties are produced, obtaining their strength largely from the mechanical interlocking of the aggregates. Asphalts are dense impervious mixtures of filler, graded aggregate and bitumen whose strengths depend mainly on the viscosity of their bitumen binder.

In the field these blacktop materials look very much the same superficially, as do the various grades of concrete, and their mix design might appear to be an even more involved business than that for concrete, embracing as it does some of the organic chemistry associated with the binder materials tar and bitumen. In fact, the design of concrete and bituminous materials have much in common — sand, graded aggregate and a cementing or binder agent. High strength asphalt is sometimes termed asphaltic concrete surfacing, which is precisely what it is. As with other structural materials, uniform output to the required standard is only achieved through control of the quality and proportions of each constituent and their combining under controlled conditions in the batching plant. Apart from the checking of the sands and aggregates, as described below, the criteria to verify in blacktop materials are the viscosity and proportion of the binder and the mixing temperature.

Clay bricks

In a country with a well established mechanised brickmaking industry the quality and uniformity of bricks can normally be relied upon to be of a high standard, conforming to the requirements of the particular grade in question. Site supervision will be mainly concerned with ensuring that the correct grade of bricks is being used and with checking that chipped or otherwise damaged bricks are rejected. Bricks can suffer in transport, especially over rough roads, and unloading methods are sometimes rough and ready, like directly dumping off a tipper lorry. Poor quality bricks will have a high water absorption rate and can suffer in frosts.

In those countries where bricks may be widely used, but which nevertheless do not have developed brick making facilities, bricks can be expected to be inferior and far from uniform. Often the bricks are crudely handmade or made with very basic equipment in hand-fired kilns. The kilns are set up wherever suitable brickmaking clays exist and the most obvious indication of the site of a kiln may be its rusty battered chimney.

Bricks produced under these conditions are, not unexpectedly, irregular in size, shape and mechanical properties. The methods of sampling and quality control used in mechanised works are not appropriate in these circumstances and a different approach is required.

Conventional quality control might be unnecessarily wasteful, leading to a rejection rate disproportionate to the quality and quantity of the local supplies available. Such local brickworks require visiting individually and only the better ones chosen. Bricks from these kilns should be sampled by the load rather than by the occasional sample, and a workable average standard established. Commonly applied tests are for weight and crushing strength, ring on striking, colour and dimensional uniformity. Bricks should also be broken open so that the core of the brick can be inspected, indicating the thoroughness or otherwise of firing in the kiln. Wise specifications should of course be written to suit the practical limitations of available supplies and methods rather than demanding an impractical standard. Nevertheless if investigations show that improvements in standards over the traditional ways can be readily achieved then these should of course be implemented. Because traditional methods have been used locally for generations it does not necessarily mean that there is no room for improvement. This philosophy should be applied to all materials and methods of production in the search for efficient economical construction.

Cement

Ordinary Portland cement is the most widely used type of cement at home or overseas, in its familiar guise or as a foreign equivalent. The form in which it is delivered to site depends very largely on the size and type of site. A small building site will probably take its deliveries in 50 kg bags, though the use of small silos is also common. Large sites will almost invariably use direct bulk cement storage in large silos.

In overseas countries where bulk cement may not be available, bagged cement has to be delivered to site by rail or truck and stored in large sheds. From the sheds the cement may be loaded into silos by conveyor, a tedious business which involves manhandling the 50 kg bags.

Cement stores should be amply sized, secure, ventilated and weatherproof structures, large enough to comfortably accommodate the stock of cement and any handling equipment. Preferably the bags should be stacked clear of the ground on pallets, though this is not practical where large quantities are involved. A more convenient practice in such cases is to sacrifice the bottom layer of bags as long as it is checked that they are not later used unscrupulously in the works. Bags should not be stacked more than about 3 m high with 4 m as the very maximum.

Where different types of cement are being used, say Ordinary Portland and Sulphate Resisting, the two should of course be kept separate with clear demarkations. At least with bagged cement it is an easy matter to identify different kinds and to estimate quickly the tonnage of each in store. A low stockpile indicates, hopefully, that a new consignment is due and it is well worthwhile inspecting new deliveries to confirm the type and tonnage arriving.

In one example on an overseas project, seven different brands of cement, each purporting to be equivalent to Ordinary Portland cement, from five countries were present in the cement store during an acute cement shortage. Being bagged, the cements were identifiable and thus their properties were able to be verified before the cements were approved for use. Careless unloading and stacking can result in high wastage from split bags, or deterioration in damaged bags and thus low quality cement being used. Spilt cement swept from the floor should be discarded. Cement stored in bags tends to go lumpy, especially if buried deep in the stockpile, however dry the store is. It becomes a matter of judgment whether to accept or reject the cement – generally if the lumps can be crushed by hand, the cement is satisfactory.

It is, as a general principle, always good practice to inspect major items as soon as they arrive on site. Inspection should be done at the time of off-loading or as soon thereafter as practical. If materials of doubtful or incorrect quality are present, then the sooner this is discovered the better.

Bulk deliveries into silos is a convenient method of accepting and storing cement, especially where large quantities are concerned, but this method of storage is not without its disadvantages.

The quantity of cement in a silo is difficult to estimate because it cannot be seen, the traditional method of banging the silo side with a lump hammer for the change of tone is approximate to say the least, and to run out of cement in mid-pour is an embarrassing experience. Where more than one type of cement is in use, a separate silo is required for each type and it may not be difficult to confuse one silo with the other and deliver cement to the wrong silo. If this occurs a decision needs to be taken whether or not to empty the offending silo, the cement need not be wasted, but it is not permitted to mix different types of cement.

Concrete blocks

Solid, cellular or hollow, concrete blocks are produced in block-making machines either at site or bought from a commercial manufacturer.

Given a good mix design and conscientious application good quality blocks are not difficult to produce. A good block will be sound, sharp edged, and dimensionally accurate, graded by its crushing strength and weight. For hollow load-bearing blocks wall thicknesses are important and all blocks should be adequately cured if they are not to crumble away in handling. As with other cement-bound materials, good control should be exercised on the storing, proportioning and mixing of the constituent materials.

Lime and plaster

These two extensively used materials, supplied in bags, should be stored in the dry.

Gypsum plaster (calcium sulphate) is used with lime mortars to form plasters and rendering.

There are two main types of lime: non-hydraulic and hydraulic. The former is manufactured from 'fat' limestone, that is limestone having a high calcium content, whilst the latter is manufactured from 'lean' limestone, which has a lower calcium content and usually contains silicates and aluminates. Non-hydraulic limes which cannot set under water, hence the name, are used to make ordinary lime mortars which are workable but structurally weak. They are also used with cement to improve the workability of cement mortars. Mortar made from inferior non-hydraulic lime may suffer from 'popping', caused by the expansion of previously unslaked particles of quick lime. Hydraulic limes, which by contrast can set under water, are structurally stronger but make less workable mortars than non-hydraulic limes.

Attention should therefore be paid to the quality of lime supplied and whether it is hydraulic or non-hydraulic, as required by the specification.

Pipes

Pipes, so commonplace, come in what may appear to be a bewildering selection of materials, each requiring special handling, laying, and jointing techniques. Even with each material type there are many grades and classes; spun concrete, reinforced concrete, prestressed concrete, asbestos-cement, salt glazed ware and vitrified clay ware, u PVC, polythene, pitch fibre, ductile, cast iron, spun iron, wrought iron, steel, etc. All pipes, however, should bear on their walls a mark of their manufacturer, and the standard and class to which they conform. These should be ascertained, often easier said than done when the pipes are covered in the dust or mud of the site, and checked against the relevant standard in order to identify correctly the pipes against the specifications. The various types of plastic pipes need close attention in this respect.

With the exception of plastic pipes, most varieties can be stored in the open. Plastic-based pipes degrade in sunlight and should therefore be kept under cover, they are also easily damaged and should be handled accordingly. Clay ware pipes are also easily damaged but most other kinds are fairly robust and can stand up to site knocks. All pipes, however, should be handled and stacked carefully in accordance with their manufacturer's recommendations to prevent damage. Very particular attention should be paid to ensuring and checking that the pipe ends are not damaged, otherwise a faulty joint will result. The ends of smaller pipes are often delivered in protective wrappings. The materials for making the joints, rings or gaskets, external collars and sleeves or solvents, should be checked for soundness or shelf life and stored safely. Joint fittings should also bear identifying marks of standard and class.

Steel pipes are often supplied as specified with internal and/or external protective coatings provided to extend the working life of the pipe in corrosive soils or atmospheres (not all pipes are buried). The linings should be inspected for soundness and any necessary repairs effected.

Sands and aggregates

A tour of inspection around the stockpiles of sands and aggregates on a site may not seem the most interesting part of supervision and yet sands and aggregates are the biggest single consumable item of many a project. They are used not only for making the obvious structural concrete of buildings, but also they are used extensively in road and pavement constructions for the surface and underlaying courses. Sand is used in mortar for laying brick and blockwork, and sands and aggregates in making concrete blocks. The cleanliness, grading and hardness of sands and aggregates materially affect the strength and durability of concrete, and so the stockpiles around a batching plant are worth more than just a passing glance.

At a batching plant the different sizes of aggregates should be separated from each other with robust walls long enough and high enough to accommodate the largest of stockpiles reasonably anticipated.

A concrete base should be laid strong enough to withstand wheel loads from loaders and wide enough to project at least beyond the compartment dividing walls. The base should be level or laid to a slight fall to the outside. Opportunity should be taken when a compartment falls empty to inspect the condition of walls and base and effect any necessary repairs. It is when stocks are low and bottom scrapings are made that contamination of aggregates can occur.

The stockpiles themselves should be inspected for cleanliness, and uniformity of grading. Dirty or irregularly graded materials usually mean trouble at the quarry or at the crushing and screening plant and a visit to either or both should be made. With practice it is possible to pick out by eye any significant changes in the supply, grading or condition of stockpiled aggregates. Each source produces materials with an individual 'set' and appearance as it sits in the stockpile, and variations become apparent in the large volumes present. A scramble up the stockpile for a closer look is usually worth the effort.

The above remarks, written with aggregate stockpiles for concrete in mind, apply equally to other stockpiled aggregates or crushed and graded stone, for example those made for road and pavement construction.

Sands, as opposed to stone aggregates, may be naturally won or made from crushed rock. Sands for mortar are different in character to those required for concrete, and are easily distinguished from them. The mortar sand stockpiles are usually much smaller and tend to be dotted around the site wherever bricklaying is in progress.

Steel reinforcement for concrete

Steel reinforcement for concrete comes in two main forms, bar and fabric. In turn, bar and fabric are manufactured in many grades.

The most usual grades of bar reinforcement used today are hot rolled plain round mild steel, hot rolled deformed bars (high yield) and cold worked bars (high yield). These grades have different compositions and properties but fortunately the bars are easily identifiable by their shape or surface. Hot rolled plain round mild steel bars are as described, the common plain round bar of mild steel. Hot rolled deformed high yield bars are usually ribbed, indented or otherwise surface deformed and have high yield, high bond properties. Cold worked bars are commonly of the square twisted type and again have high yield high bond properties.

Bar reinforcement is delivered to site usually in standard 12 m lengths, though 18 m lengths can be supplied if requested, or ready cut, bent and labelled from the suppliers. As 12 m is longer than many lorries, it is common for the 12 m bundles of steel to be doubled over before loading. This is not detrimental to the majority of the bars' length though the section immediately next to the fold, especially on a tight radius, should not be used in permanent works. Steel bar is subject to a good deal of rough handling before it reaches its final destination in the works, for instance being dragged to location by tractor. Again this is generally not detrimental though care must be taken with high yield steel in extremely cold temperatures where brittleness may be present.

The steel is stacked at the steel yard which should be hard surfaced, plane and well drained. Ideally steel should be stacked off the ground, preferably continuously supported though this is seldom practical. If timber spacers are used they should be closely spaced to provide uniform support and to prevent the heavy steel bundles deforming under their own weight.

Unless supply is a problem it is unusual to find two different types of high yield steel being used on the same site, normally plain mild steel and one type of high yield steel is found. On overseas sites where supply may be difficult from time to time it may be considered necessary to purchase whatever steel is currently available locally. This is a doubtful practice as there is little chance of establishing the steel's origin or characteristics. There may perhaps be a case for using the unproven steel in non-structural situations and it can do no harm in uncritical temporary works. The great danger, however, is that once on site, the unidentifiable steel will become mixed with approved steel and be built into the permanent works and for this reason alone such purchases must be viewed with extreme caution. The question of permitting sub-standard or unproven materials of whatever kind on site as a temporary expedient, or for temporary works only, is fraught with dangers, the main one being, of course, that once on site there is always the risk that such materials will, however inadvertently, be incorporated into the permanent works. They may or may not then be retrievable but invariably dispute and disruption ensues. Very careful consideration should therefore be given to this question before such materials are permitted on, or permitted to remain on site.

Each different grade of steel should be stacked separately to avoid wrong use, even with different surface forms mistakes can be made and the wrong grade of steel used in the wrong place. If the steel arrives ready cut, bent and labelled, a check should be made to see that the labels are metal, clearly marked in waterproof ink or crayon and securely attached to their respective bundles. Without labels one bundle of steel, straight or bent is easily mistaken for a similar bundle meant for perhaps another beam or column. It is remarkable, though, how from the disarray of a steel yard, with its apparent haphazard stacks of steel, gas cylinders and burning gear, orderly fixed correct reinforcement almost invariably results.

The cutting to length by burning of mild steel bars does not normally adversely affect the steel's properties, but physical damage should of course be avoided. High yield and other special steels should always be cropped to length, not flame cut. The bending of bars by hand or by mechanical means on the bar bending machine is, however, a more likely source of damage. Bending to too tight a radius or bending too quickly may cause a bar to split or flake. An inspection of bars for these defects should be made periodically, and a general look around the steel yard for evidence of bad practice, or bad steel, is recommended.

Steel bar is often received on site in a clean unrusted condition and, as long as it is not oily, can be fixed directly in the works. However, it normally lies stacked for a while during which time it rusts and, whilst a certain amount of rust is tolerable and even beneficial, excessive rust is unacceptable. Not only does rust produce a loose surface reducing bond, but it erodes the cross section of the bar. Bars affected thus should be scraped or blast cleaned and, if necessary, down graded. At the other extreme, bars stacked in countries prone to sand storms are likely to become polished by the sand and may then require spraying to induce rust for bond.

Steel fabric reinforcement is normally supplied in mats 4.8 m x 2.4 m of plain round, indented or otherwise deformed, hard drawn steel wire or cold worked deformed steel bar steel, produced to standardised weights, bar diameters and bar spacing.

The mesh size and bar diameters vary from type to type, long mesh, square mesh and structural fabric being the common structural patterns whilst wrapping fabric is used for non-structural applications.

Long mesh is extensively used for reinforcing concrete roads and pavements, square mesh is used, for example, as general ground floor slab reinforcement and structural fabric may be used as a direct alternative to bar reinforcement in suspended slabs.

With works' produced mesh, the bars are electrically welded at their intersections and a high quality product is achieved. Points to watch for, nevertheless, are good welding and an absence of burning of the bars. Where justified, say if a non-standard mesh is required, the fabric may be produced on site and then inspection of the two above points becomes more important. Check also the bar spacings and diameters. Because fabric generally utilises smaller diameter bars, cutting and trimming is usually done by cropping rather than burning. Fabric should preferably be stacked off the ground.

Wrapping fabric, supplied in mats 2.4 m x 1.2 m, is made of small diameter mild steel bars and is used, for example, as reinforcement in such applications as steel beam and column encasements and similar 'non-structural' situations.

The steel used in prestressed concrete work is described later in the section on prestressed concrete construction, pages 149-150.

Structural steelwork

Structural steelwork, the subject of chapter 6, is briefly mentioned here because any list of major construction materials would be incomplete without it.

In contrast to *in-situ* reinforced concrete, which is generally a site-made mixture of different ingredients each of which is controlled from site and consequently involves a large commitment of site supervision in its making, structural steelwork arrives at site ready made and site supervision is concentrated on its erection. With steel the quality controls for ingredients and properties are effected at the steelworks, for standard sizes in the rolling mills, and for fabrication in the fabricator's yard.

There are numerous types of steel but the steel that is most commonly used for structural work is that to BS 4360 'Weldable Structural Steel', in one of its three grades 43, 50 or 55. The first, grade 43, is the most widely used. If structural steels of different grades are present on site they should be kept separate and bear clear identifying marks.

Despite their strength, structural steel components are frequently damaged during loading, transporting, unloading and stacking. Light section assemblies, for example roof trusses, are especially vulnerable but thoughtless stacking on lorry or in the yard can cause damage to the most robust of sections. Damaged items should be noted and repaired, or replaced if irreparable.

The arrival of each individual item should be checked off and entered on a drawing or similar record sheet for future reference, programming and measurement purposes.

These aspects, and many others, are dealt with more fully in chapter 6 Structural Steelwork.

Timber

The grading, selection, and specification of timber is an involved science because of the hundreds of available timber species and wide variations within any one species. As far as site control is concerned a common sense visual inspection of the timber as stored on site should be adequate to determine its suitability for use as far as general joinery and simple structural work is concerned.

Timber for major load-bearing structures, however, requires the stringent examination and testing of each individual piece of timber. Random sampling is not sufficient.

The physical defects most commonly found in general sawn timber are knots, waney edges, warping, splits, and shakes. These are more or less serious depending on their number, position and extent, and recommendations exist giving guidance on their acceptance or rejection. Knots and warping are well known. A waney edge is the natural chamfer sometimes present on otherwise square edged sections. Shakes and splits are types of split, shakes are fissures extending along the grain, splits extend from face to face.

Site facilities

Batching plants

Batching plants, as opposed to 'mixers', are usually established for the production of large quantities of uniform, good quality concrete and other cement-bound materials, bituminous macadams and asphalts.

The plants may be established at site or at the works of an external supplier. Whichever is the case, the principles of inspection, though not perhaps the convenience, remain the same.

Two aspects of concrete batching plants which require inspection are, firstly, the mechanical plant itself and, secondly, the material stockpiles. Of the machinery, the important items to check are the weight batching mechanisms and the calibrations for water, aggregates and cement. For blacktop plants the bitumen and temperature controls need checking.

In the case of concrete batching, additives may be specified in which case the apparatus for gauging and dispensing the additives should be checked.

Points to observe in stockpile inspections are noted on page 44.

Contractor's stores

This establishment will resemble the store of a builders' merchant, housing in a secure building or outside in a fenced compound the multitude of miscellaneous small, and not so small, items required for the project. A walk around the store will enable a check to be made on the items whose availability, or absence, may affect the progress of the works. A check can also be made on the grade of goods supplied and whether they have been received in good condition and are being stored correctly — badly stored goods could deteriorate and become unusable, perhaps entailing a delay until replacements are supplied. Rubber and plastic water bar and gaskets, for example, need careful storing to avoid damage or deterioration, so do paints, solvents, adhesives and other chemicals. Special storage areas may in fact be necessary for these latter categories and special fire precautions provided.

Examples of common building materials which might be required for a project but which are not considered separately in this book are: boards and slabs, miscellaneous ferrous and non-ferrous castings and fittings, glass ware, clay ware, roof and decorative tiles, and ceramics.

All such items would be subject to sample approval, specification check, and manufacturer's/supplier's test certificates. Manufacturer's test certificates are normally required for all permanent materials incorporated in the works, to show that the materials comply with the appropriate specification and are prepared by independent laboratories or materials testing establishments. They provide a means of checking that materials meet the specification without the need for elaborate and extensive testing facilities at site. If the quality of a product is in question, reference to the Contractor's purchase order and a check on the relevant test certificate should provide the answer.

The laboratory

On a busy site the laboratory will be one of the busiest offices, provided with its own transport and working day and night shifts if the situation demands. It is in the laboratory that the quality of materials and construction, whether supplied from external sources or site-produced, is tested and monitored. Dependent on the type and size of contract, a laboratory could have a soils section, concrete section, blacktop section and a general materials section for example. The soils section would be responsible for the investigation of soils, their characteristics and classifications and the sampling and testing of field construction. The concrete section would test cement and aggregates individually and as mixed in fresh concrete and organise the making and testing of cubes and cylinders for the proving of hardened concrete. In the blacktop section, bituminous materials, aggregates and fillers would be sampled and tested individually and as laid in bituminous macadam and asphaltic construction. Cores would be taken to investigate the soundness of in-built construction and solvents used to determine, by analysis, the accuracy or otherwise of the proportioning of the constituents. The monitoring of standards in all the major construction disciplines

49

involves the taking and testing of hundreds or even thousands of samples as work progresses, and imposes a heavy repetitive workload on the laboratory which must be staffed accordingly. The information arising from these tests is recorded on graphs and charts as described in chapter 2, Records.

Another major function of the laboratory is to receive, examine and report on samples of the manufactured items supplied for incorporation in the permanent works. On a project such as a new terminal building for a major airport, the number of building and architectural samples would be high and could include ceiling and wall cladding panels, bricks, glass, tiles and fabrics, paints, floor coverings, door furniture, etc.

Approved or not, it is a good practice to label and record these samples and keep them on display so that comparisons can be made against new or similar items from the same or other sources. The same principle of approved and not approved samples is also applied to items manufactured on site, for example brick panels and pointing, precast blocks and other precast items. Samples resulting from investigatory or exploratory work, for example soil samples from boreholes, aggregate samples and cores cut from concrete or asphaltic construction, should also be kept in the laboratory. It is salutary if examples of bad construction are kept to demonstrate what is not required, what must be avoided, what can happen if inspection is not thorough. All samples, to be any use, must be labelled and fully described.

It is preferable that all samples should be kept in the laboratory and fully referenced. Usually though the more relevant ones are found scattered about section offices, usually on the floor and barely referenced, because a laboratory is a working office, not a museum.

It is common to find two similarly equipped laboratories on site, one operated by the Inspector and the other by the Contractor. This seeming perhaps unnecessary duplication of facilities is justified by the requirements in the one case for the Inspector's responsibility to monitor construction standards and in the other by the Contractor's responsibility and wishes to construct to a specified standard and his commercial interest in constructing economically. There is usually good co-operation between the respective staffs.

Quarry and crushing plant

Stone quarries and crushing plants producing road stone or sand and aggregate for concrete are more often than not situated remote from the sites they serve. Nevertheless, wherever practicable, they should be visited during the duration of a contract, the opportunity to do so being made or taken as appropriate, even if it entails a day's journey and the overcoming of a reluctance to be absent from pressing business on site. They will in any case need approval as a source of supply before their products are used in the works. The solution to problems with aggregate shape and size may lie in the blasting procedure used at the quarry. Primary crushing and screening may be carried out at the quarry and secondary crushing and screening at a more central depot or perhaps even on site itself if convenient. The quarry and plant may belong to the Contractor or an independent owner, government or private.

A quarry will probably appear of little interest to an observer, just a rather large hole in a hillside, perhaps terraced and with a rough road leading to the face. There are, however, certain points which should be checked during inspection. The overburden should have been stripped back well clear of the top of the quarry face to prevent it contaminating the stone to be quarried; the stone as exposed in the faces of the quarry should be inspected for such points as soundness, uniformity, bedding and inclusions which could affect the quality of stone extracted; the general set up, safety precautions, storage of explosives, condition of mechanical plant, loaders, dump trucks, crusher conveyers and screens.

Observe how well, or otherwise, the mechanical plant, especially the loaders and trucks, is maintained.

The major maintenance facilities may be at the quarry/screening plant or elsewhere at a central plant depot. Note the extent of the plant, is it sufficient to deliver the quantities of stone demanded by the project?

If new haul roads are required between quarry and site, they should be designed generously to cope with the estimated volume of haul traffic. For a major project this could be a formidable amount. If use has to be made of the existing road system, then upgrading of sections of road, bridges, or limiting restrictions on lorry weight or number may be necessary. For efficient haulage operations, haul roads should be regularly inspected and maintained. On many large projects stone is conveyed by rail.

The condition of the crushers, conveyor screens, and washing plant, at the main crushing and screening plant should be closely examined. A rackety plant will produce irregularly graded aggregates as these plants have an arduous life and require constant maintenance. The size and speed of the conveyor belts should be equated to the overall capacity of the plant and the motors and the screens should be inspected for damage. Torn screens cannot possibly produce uniformly graded stone. Again, inspect the stockpiles of the various sized aggregates and sands, the remarks concerning inspection of site stockpiles apply equally to stockpiles at the screening plant. In addition, samples of stone from the stockpiles at the screening plant and at site should be compared to see whether the stone degrades during loading, transportation and re-stockpiling.

51

Gravel, used 'as-dug', or crushed and screened is often found in extensive beds, above or below the ground water table and is fairly readily won.

The principle of supervision at source is a most important one and the earlier in the process line it is started the better. Guidance has already been given on the inspection of current stocks at site but, applying the same principle, visits should be made from time to time, to the cement works, and to the quarries from where the raw materials for cement, limestone and clay, are obtained. The earlier in the process line, the less frequent need be the inspections from site, other controls being exercised by the various intervening manufacturers and processors.

4 Elements of Construction

This chapter consists of an alphabetical list of the more common elements and divisions of construction and explains what is important to check, the techniques and methods of inspection and how to set about inspection. The underlying factor is to have an appreciation of the design principles involved and to look for their application in practice. For example, the main steel reinforcement in a concrete cantilever lies in the top of the section, for a column base in the bottom; compacting a layer of fill by six or even twelve passes is a waste of effort if the moisture content is incorrect; incorrectly bonded brickwork is unstable; stone pitching or stone walls will soon collapse if only shallow flat stones are used in their construction, through stones are required to tie the construction together; so know the principle, look for the pattern.

Many of the elements covered refer especially to concrete construction and are written with this in mind. Where other materials or types of construction are involved these are self evident or, again, the text applies equally to these other technologies.

Standard proving or performance tests, for example pile bearing tests, borehole pumping tests, and pipe pressure and watertightness tests are usually particularly covered in the project specifications, and standard procedures have been developed over the years.

The elements of construction considered in this chapter are:

Arches, domes and vaults
Beams
Blacktop construction
Boreholes (for water supply)
Brickwork and blockwork
Bridges (simple)
Cantilevers
Carcassing
Cement-bound granular materials
Columns
Concrete paving
Drains and drainage
Fencing
Formwork and shuttering
Foundations
Glass block walls
Handrailing and walkways
Inserts

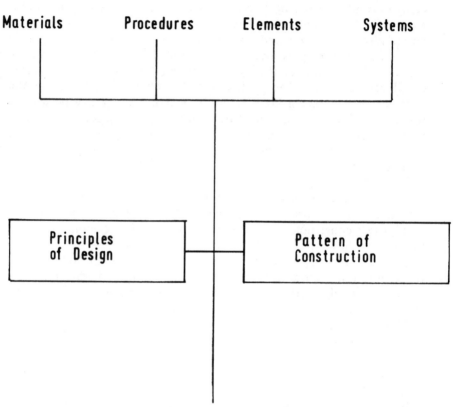

ELEMENTS OF CONSTRUCTION

Materials   Procedures   Elements   Systems

Principles
of Design

Pattern of
Construction

line, level, security, strength, before, during, after construction

Diagram 4

In-situ concrete
Joint fillers
Joint sealers
Kerbs and paving slabs
Masonry
Mechanical and electrical installations
Paints and painting
Piling
Plasters, renders and screeds
Precast construction
Precast yard
Pressure grouting
Reinforcement
Retaining walls
Roofing and flooring
Secondary steelwork
Services (buried)
Services (mounted)
Setting out
Slabs
Stairs
Tanking and waterproofing
Timber components
Water bar

Arches, domes and vaults

Before construction of these items begins, it is most important to check that setting out, centering and profile are accurately and securely fixed and marked. Abutments and springings, too, should be checked for trueness in all respects, otherwise errors, perhaps difficult to correct as construction progresses, will be introduced.

During construction ensure that erection progresses evenly and symmetrically across the structure so that line is kept and uneven loads on falsework or supports avoided.

Where reinforced concrete is the construction material, shells are comparatively thin and care should be taken in placing and compacting the concrete and in ensuring that the reinforcement is not displaced. These difficulties are made worse if the slope of the shell demands a top shutter. It is better by far if top shutters can be avoided by suitable mix design or casting procedures.

In masonry or brickwork construction adherence to the setting out and the bonding of the courses should be maintained at all times to achieve even courses and a coherent structure. These materials form a stable structure only on completion of construction.

Because structures like arches, domes and vaults are nowadays often used to achieve a striking architectural effect, care should be

55

taken of the surface faces to prevent their becoming damaged under construction. Removal of shutters and falsework should be carried out carefully and the surfaces protected from damage by subsequent operations.

Beams

Beams may be unstable in their newly erected condition, relying on a topping slab or, as yet, unconstructed diaphragms for their eventual stability. They may require temporary support laterally, longitudinally or from beneath. Over toppling, especially, is a danger to be guarded against. Bearings, plain or fancy, should be complete to accept the beams.

Blacktop construction

The most important factor to get right when laying and rolling blacktop is the temperature (cold construction excepted of course). If this is correct the material will usually roll out satisfactorily. Inspect the surface during rolling and note any high spots, waves and signs of surface cracking or unravelling. Successive rolling will usually eliminate these initial defects but if it does not the defective areas will eventually require cutting out and relaying. The relative ease in which defective areas may be replaced is one advantage of blacktop construction.

Check the layer for thickness as laid and rolled, if there are succeeding layers then any reasonable short fall in thickness may be made up in these succeeding layers which will be of equal or superior quality. A check should also be made on the condition and level of the surface on which the particular layer in question is to be laid. High spots should be graded off whilst filling of low spots may be necessary. It is important to ensure that in the layered construction, as used for roads and pavements, each individual layer is correct to level and surface tolerance before the succeeding layer is laid. If this is not done difficulty will be encountered in laying the surface layer to final tolerance, and remember that tolerances get tighter from bottom to top.

Check the surface for level and laying tolerance. Relative levels are more important to observe than absolute levels, but it is important to maintain the laying tolerances of the plane surface as required by the specification.

Joints, end or side, should be cut back square to sound material before laying continuation or adjacent strips. Joints should be staggered, side and end, in successive vertical layers, and primed.

Observe the type and weight of rollers and the rolling pattern being used and check that these comply with the approved contract work statement, but bear in mind also that rolling methods may be changed in the light of experience gained in full-scale construction.

Field trials are usually specified before full-scale construction in order to determine rolling procedures. Once these procedures have been approved they should not be changed without permission. Observe too the behaviour of the material under rolling, it should bed down nicely under successive passes and experience will soon train the eye to judge how things are going.

Regarding mechanical plant, check that the paver is in good working condition, especially the level control device and the material spreader screws. Ensure that there are sufficient lorries available to deliver a continuous supply of material to the paver.

Blacktop construction cannot proceed in the rain or on wet surfaces so check that the laying surface is adequately dry before construction commences. The surface should also be kept clear of mud from lorry tyres or from other construction plant.

Boreholes (for water supply)

Water supply boreholes, as installed, are a mixture of civil, mechanical, and electrical engineering and here the civil content only is described.

Sinking the borehole should be accompanied by careful recording of the strata encountered, the water table level, and the depth achieved.

Before the lining and well screen are installed, inspect the physical condition of each, paying particular attention to the screens. Check that they are undamaged, located in the agreed position in the tube's length and are of the agreed extent.

Filter material placed to surround the inserted lining should be checked for cleanliness and grading, and for volume placed.

On completion the top of the borehole should be covered securely for safety and to prevent ingress of dirt, pending insertion of the pump and tube, associated equipment and construction of the well house.

Brickwork and blockwork

Supervision of construction in these two materials has much in common though blockwork, being of a coarser nature, may often be considered only on structural merit whereas brickwork has both a structural and an architectural role.

Common matters to observe are the correct provision of wall ties whether between adjacent leaves or between wall panels and framing eg blockwork panel to surrounding concrete frames; the inclusion of horizontal or vertical reinforcement where specified; damp proof courses undamaged; that sufficient detail is applied to joints, especially that expansion joints are free; that cavities are kept clear of debris; that lintols whether precast or *in-situ* are properly made and seated and the correct way up; and that bonding, courses and bed joints and perpends are neatly made and kept. Check too that the motar mix being used is the correct one and that the bricks or blocks themselves are not damaged.

Attention should be paid, when facing bricks are being laid, that access scaffolding does not damage the bricks and that the brick face is not marked by unsightly mortar droppings, in other words that the appearance of the brick face is not spoiled by thoughtless construction sequences.

The top surfaces of unfinished walls should be protected from the weather during construction. Remember that fresh mortar, like fresh concrete, is susceptible to frost.

Bridges (simple)

The construction of simple bridges presents no particular difficulty, following normal construction procedures.

Certain matters peculiar to bridges should be observed at the appropriate time as construction progresses and these are reviewed below.

Pay particular attention to the soundness and security of foundations and abutments. Ensure, for example, that any anti-scour provisions are constructed to the full design outlines and not skimped.

Backfill against the abutments should be most thoroughly and uniformly compacted. One of the most common defects in bridge construction is differential settlement between the bridge structure itself and the fill behind the abutments. Even with the most thorough compaction some differential settlement is almost inevitable, so no effort should be spared in this important matter − resist any short cutting attempts. Check that bearings are true, clean and in good repair.

Check that designed cambers are properly effected.

All required clearances, access lighting, headroom, etc, should be safely maintained at all times during construction, most especially if there is a public right of way or other public access to be observed.

During construction constantly check the accuracy and security of all falsework and centering.

Cantilevers

During erection, stresses in cantilevers particularly may be different from those for which the finished structure may be designed to withstand. This is especially true for *in-situ* concrete where support is continuous during casting and needs to remain so to the day that the props are removed, the danger being that a simply supported condition may otherwise occur. Propped cantilevers are a special case and need even greater attention. In all instances, a knowledge of the design is required before construction proceeds.

Carcassing

The term encompasses all the many fitting-out activities which convert an empty structure to a working building. A sound practical knowledge of many trades is required if supervision is to be more than superficial. Recognition of, and insistence on, good workmanship are essential tools.

As carcassing proceeds so too does the danger of damage to completed work, carcassing being very much an exercise in completion. Insist that adequate precautions are taken to protect the finished work from subsequent damage, deliberate or accidental.

Prior to carcassing, cladding will have been completed. In order to avoid, or at least minimise, undesirable wind effects within and upon the building, cladding should proceed to an agreed sequence.

Cement-bound granular materials

Covered in this section are such materials as dry lean concrete, soil cement and other cement-bound granular materials.

With these materials it is the mixing, grading and cement content which are crucial to sound construction. Cement and water weights are controlled at the batching plant. Aggregate weights are controlled at the batching plant and it may be necessary to exercise additional control of quality at the place of aggregate winning and screening. It is also necessary to control the elapsed time between mixing and compacting in order to avoid partially set material being used.

In laying and rolling, observe how the material behaves. It should remain coherent and roll to form a stable surface without unravelling or surface cracking. Check that the desired thickness is achieved, though it is usually permissible for any reasonable shortfall to be made up in the immediately succeeding layer of superior material. Ensure that the freshly laid material is emulsion sprayed to cure and that site traffic is kept off for the specified interval after laying.

Check that edges are satisfactorily cut back to sound material before adjacent widths are cast against the existing construction.

As laid quality is conveniently monitored by densities of the compacted material, though crushing strengths are also measured.

As with blacktop construction, the rollers and rolling procedures should be as approved in trials or following subsequent experience. Mechanical plant should be in good working order.

Columns

Columns may require supporting temporarily in the interval between erection and connection to permanent framing members. Before the permanent connections are made plumb, line and level should be verified. Seating cleats are required for framing in prefabricated elements or starter bars for *in-situ* construction. Completed free standing columns are vulnerable to site vehicular damage and should be protected as well as possible.

Concrete paving

The laying of concrete pavements is a highly mechanical process and when trouble arises it is more often than not of a mechanical rather than a materials nature. Verify that the batching plant, delivery lorries, the elements of the paving train and concrete vibrators are in good working order. If a night shift is in operation, check the number and adequacy of the lights.

Side forms should be robust, well fastened down to withstand the weight of the paving train and its vibrations, and be true to line and level. Badly bent forms make for bad paving joints in the length of the forms and at joints between adjacent forms. In adjusting for level ensure that significant grout loss cannot occur beneath the forms if packing to level is necessary, and that any packing is firm.

Designed joints in the pavement should be checked for spacing and correct detailing, there are several types but the pattern of jointing is repetitive and it is where exceptions occur that mistakes can be made. Crack-inducing battens should be securely fastened down to prevent their displacement, dowel bar assemblies should be secure, and projecting dowel bars should be truly square to the face from which they project.

During casting pay special attention to compaction of the concrete adjacent to joints, these areas are often additionally vibrated by hand because of their congested nature.

Completed work should be covered and protected as soon as practical; no matter what the precautions, the odd stray animal and occasional pedestrian usually manage to leave a trail of footmarks in the fresh concrete. Joint grooves are best cut when the concrete is hard enough not to tear under the cutting discs yet green enough to cut easily. Joint cutting should in any event be completed promptly otherwise uncontrolled cracking of the concrete will occur, the very action the joints are designed to prevent.

Strict control of formwork striking is important otherwise care will give way to haste and damage to the concrete will ensue. This damage will almost certainly be to the concrete edges rather than to its surface, and the resulting damaged joint lines will be unsightly and, much more serious, give rise to defective joints. The striking of side forms off dowelled joints is a difficult operation. In the extreme, if too much leverage is exerted on the dowels, the dowels will crack the green concrete in which they are embedded, thus destroying the joint.

Drains and drainage

The points to check when inspecting drainage runs are line and level, fall, bedding and joints and connections to manholes and similar structures. One objective way to approach drain laying is to consider it as an exercise in assembling precast units to specified line and level, and requiring sound joints. A well executed drainage layout is a matter of some satisfaction.

Gravity drains are generally laid from the low end upwards with sockets uphill. It is as well to walk the route before laying commences to check that there are no obvious obstructions to the line as shown on the drawings. Trial pits *en route* are a good idea if existing services are known or anticipated. Existing services can cause problems and it is awkward if a new and existing service clash with no tolerance in fall for adjustments.

Drains should be laid in a straight line between manholes. Linearity may be checked by illuminating one end and viewing the circle from the other.

In checking levels it is the relative, rather than the absolute, which is important. Correcting drain levels to precisely those shown on the drawings is usually impractical and unnecessary.

Falls should automatically follow from levels when laying and minimum falls should be checked, this is especially relevant when making unavoidable alterations to line to avoid obstructions.

Pipes with broken backs are one of the commonest examples of pipe failure. It is essential for pipes without a concrete surround that the pipes are evenly bedded throughout their length. The most common culprits are the hard packings used temporarily to support the pipes and bring them up to level, these should be removed after laying of the pipe bedding material. Other hard spots should also be removed.

Because many pipes derive structural strength from the material that surrounds them it is important to see that trench width is kept to the minimum specified and that the surrounding material is well compacted during backfilling.

Joints require making well. Check that the correct detail has been used where pipes enter or leave manholes or structures. Flexible joints are usually provided in these locations to cope with differential settlements.

If flexible jointed pipes are provided with a concrete surround check that the flexibility has been maintained across the concrete surround. Where pipes have a concrete surround see that the pipes are secured against flotation forces caused by the upthrust from the wet concrete.

Plastic pipes should be protected from the sun when lying in their trench or stacked alongside.

During the regrading of open channel drainage check that the bank slopes remain stable and that any existing bridges and culverts *en route* are adequate for the new flows and wide enough to accommodate the new profile. Such structures will almost certainly need clearing out but should not be undermined.

Large diameter pipes can be inspected from inside, on foot or by means of special trolley. Always verify that it is safe to do so before venturing down long pipe lines. Completed drain runs lying in open trench may be displaced if the trench is flooded.

Fencing

The ubiquitious fence, spaced around the site or across country, deserves more attention than it usually receives. Much detailed work is involved in the construction of a fence and a clumsily erected one will not only look awful but also can only be made good by dismantling and re-erection — localised corrections will only make matters worse.

With post and wire fences, supervision should concentrate on the firmness of the posts in the ground and the tautness of the wires. If these are achieved a good fence will usually result. The levels of the finished fence, heights of posts, and spacing of wires need to be checked, as do the miscellaneous fastenings and fittings which connect the wires to the posts.

Inspect the posts for damage. Concrete posts are particularly vulnerable to spalling and cracking whereas timber posts are generally satisfactory. Steel posts should be well painted or galvanised otherwise corrosion soon sets in. Steel fittings should similarly be corrosion resistant and so too should be all wires and mesh.

In timber fencing, stringers, panelling, rails and posts all need soundly joining and jointing. The fences, being heavy, require firmly bedded posts. Check that weathering is effected.

If fence posts are set in concrete the concrete should not be skimped, but see also that the concrete base cannot be undermined or an unstable post will result.

Where fences border a stream they should be set back a reasonable distance from the bank top to avoid being undermined but if too much room is allowed the landowner may complain of his loss of ground. Check too on local conventions regarding which side of a hedge or ditch a fence should be erected and on which side of the posts the fence face or wires should go.

The skill required in hanging a gate properly is often underestimated, as too is the weight of a gate. Gate posts should be very firmly set, usually with a concrete base, and the gate hung and adjusted to swing and fasten easily.

Formwork and shuttering

Shuttering should be strong enough both vertically and horizontally to withstand the pressures from the wet concrete deposited within them (remembering that sometimes concrete comes with a rush from a suddenly opened skip), and to withstand rough usage from the concrete gang and knocks from a skip. Stop ends for construction joints should be secure and reasonably grout tight, this is awkward to achieve around projecting reinforcement. Any significant grout loss will result in honeycombing at the joint thus weakening an already potentially vulnerable plane.

Folding wedges used in level or other adjustments should be nailed to avoid slippage.

Great care should be taken in striking shutters, both as regards avoiding damage to the surface and edges of the concrete and also as regards striking intervals. Striking the side shutters of a beam is usually permitted before the striking of the soffit shutters, and this is safe enough provided that the shutters are so constructed that removal of the sides is possible without disturbing the soffit shutters. However where props are required to remain after soffit shutters are removed, it is not satisfactory to remove all such props in order to enable removal of the soffit shutters, and then to replace the props. If this is done permanent damage may easily be caused to the beam whilst it is in the unpropped condition.

It is safer to leave soffit shutters and props in place until the specified time for prop removal has elapsed.

An alternative solution, but one less satisfactory, to ensure partial propping whilst removing the soffit shutters, is to remove the shutters in sections if the shutter construction permits.

Depending on the importance of the section in question the shutter assembly as a whole should be checked for plumb, square, line and level, centering, tightness of joints and closure with the kicker of a previous lift. Scaffolding, props, falsework, etc, should be checked for strength and security before, during and after concreting operations. It is especially important to check that vertical props are securely founded, and not precariously perched on miscellaneous timber packings. Column shutters should be checked for plumb using theodolite, plumbline or carpenter's level before, during and after concreting.

As well as containing reinforcement, shutters often contain built-in items such as water bar, electrical conduit, sockets for surface fixings, etc. These are described under separate sections. Suffice it to record here that any check on shutters should include a check on whether built-in items are required. Shutters should also be checked for cleanliness. Binding wire, sawdust, shavings, etc, should be removed, usually by compressed air, before concreting is permitted.

This operation is fairly simple in floor slabs but can be difficult in deep beams, columns and heavily reinforced areas.

Timber shutters are the most common type being reasonably tough and easy to handle, easily constructed and easily repaired. In hot weather the timber may shrink, causing gaps which should be sealed. This can be remedied by spraying the outside of the shutters with water. Internal faces of shutters require oiling with shutter oil to prevent concrete/shutter adhesion and to facilitate striking. When a smooth finish is required to the concrete, timber shutters are sometimes lined with veneer, hardboard or similar smooth material. These produce a satisfactory finish but wear quickly and then need replacing in whole rather than in part; patching is reflected in the finished concrete surface. The lining should be securely backed otherwise a wavy surface will result.

Steel shutters are employed where many uses and/or a smooth finish is required and are excellent in this respect. In their use, however, attention should be paid to the following points.

In hot weather the shutters can become excessively hot making handling and working uncomfortable. In wet weather the shutters rust and can cause staining to concrete faces unless kept well oiled. Dents and bumps are difficult to straighten and unwanted holes should be closed by plugging welding and grinding to a smooth finish. Mating edges should be true for a close joint, they can only be drawn tight to a limited degree by bolting, so a compressible gasket or cover strip may be required. Closing onto a concrete face, for example a column kicker or previous lift, also needs care to ensure a tight joint and to avoid damaging the existing concrete. A common fault is to over estimate the strength of steel shutters. Despite their being steel they still require attention in assembly, bolting up, bracing, propping and tieing as appropriate, otherwise slippage or unacceptable deformations may occur.

Foundations

The formation should be clean and firm before base construction starts.

It is usual for soil tests to be taken to ascertain the actual soil strengths against the strengths assumed in the design calculations. In concrete construction starter bars for columns or tie beams are required or, alternatively, holding-down fastenings for prefabricated superstructure. Any built-in fixings should be correctly orientated with respect to the superstructure. Check if sulphate resisting cement, or other special cement, waterproofing or tanking, is required in buried concrete work.

Glass block walls

Heavy and easily damaged, glass blocks need strong rigid supports as well as resilient beddings, and these are the points to inspect during construction.

Handrailing and walkways

Perhaps contrary to general belief, these are not minor items to be quickly erected at the tail end of the job. More often than not they are what make a structure safe for use. Without them operation may not be permissible or life lost, perhaps, if failure were to occur.

All connections — screwed, welded, bolted, cast in, etc — should be inspected and tested for strength and stability. Undue deflections are unacceptable even if structurally safe. One test of an access is whether or not it feels safe in use.

Alignment is probably quite adequately checked by eye, most items being prefabricated to standard heights and section. Inspect the standard of fabrication and have remedied any poor workmanship in forming or finish. Sharp edges should be ground smooth and defects in protective treatments made good.

Inserts

Inserts built into shutters prior to casting should be most securely fixed. The best method is to fasten the item to the face of the shutter by screws or other positive fixings, care being taken to ensure that the item is correctly orientated when in position and not handed or skewed.

The common method of fixing inserts to the reinforcement and wedging them against the inside face of the shutter without positive fixing thereto is not recommended. Concrete placing and vibration will almost invariably cause the item to shift and move away from the shutter face, making it difficult to locate when the shutters are struck. Defacement of the concrete usually occurs in the subsequent search for the item. Apart from the need to be securely held against the shutter face, hollow items, such as boxes and conduit, should be fixed to prevent flotation and should have their ends sealed to prevent ingress of grout. They should be sufficiently robust to withstand the rigours of casting without damage; pouring concrete is a rough business.

All inserts are usually not shown on one drawing. Maybe three or four drawings need to be consulted and this is particularly true where services are concerned. It is useful, as well as wise, to prepare a schedule of inserts for each phase of construction.

In-situ concrete

The particular principles of *in-situ* concrete construction are known well enough and certain facets are discussed separately under individual headings but here a few words about general principles and the more common causes of trouble.

Concrete is a versatile material which can stand rough handling but which nevertheless can be adversely affected if certain simple rules are not followed. Being a site-produced material, manufactured under controlled conditions, its constituent materials are controlled at the batching plant to produce the required strengths, and the production mix is not achieved without extensive prior testing of trial mixes. It is a pity then if much of the careful work in mix production is negated by a careless approach to casting or the protection of the green concrete. For instance, adding excessive water to a mix to make it more manageable, and so save effort in placing, is one common malpractice and results in a weaker concrete more prone to cracking; clumsy depositing of concrete in the shutters can damage the reinforcement mats or even the shutters themselves; inattention to curing and protecting the freshly cast concrete from sun and wind can result in serious cracking; premature removal of supporting formwork can cause damage and even collapse. Unlike structual steelwork which arrives on site ready made and ready for use, concrete cannot be considered ready for use as soon as it is cast, in the case of beams it may well be ten to fourteen days before the props are removed. So, attention should not cease when the shutters are filled.

Now a few notes about joints and curing.

Joints should be checked for the following
Scabbling.
Tightness of seal between adjacent shutters.
Tightness of seal between shutters and supporting concrete.
Tightness of seal between shutters and projecting items eg water bar, reinforcement.
The provision of chamfers.
Absence of spalled edges.

Curing is an activity which needs constant surveillance to ensure that it is being applied correctly, or even applied at all. Remember that a drying wind at night can be just as dangerous as a hot daytime sun for prematurely drying out fresh concrete. If hessian is used, see that it is kept constantly damp and that it adequately covers the concrete. Polythene sheeting is an effective material but does not protect against frost. Spray-on curing membranes are similarly useful but check that they have enough body and are effective for long enough, do not stain the concrete, and do not adversely affect later work.

Joint fillers

Compressible joint fillers should be fixed securely and squarely against the face of the joint they line. If this is not done the filler will become displaced during concreting and a solid, or even vacant joint, can result. Check that any ribs or fins are cut back to the main joint face before securing the filler and that the filler is fastened back tightly to prevent grout penetrating between it and the face. Ensure that the filler is carefully fitted around such items as water bars or dowel bars projecting from the joint face. Check that the filler is the correct thickness for the joint being formed and that correct allowance has been made for a joint sealer along the top and/or edge of the joint.

Joint sealers

The application of joint sealers in concrete construction is often left until late, often too late, in a contract by which time the joint grooves are full of dirt or stone and their edges chipped and broken. Sealing is often carried out intermittently and, on extensive projects like airfields, necessarily remote from the central site office, sometimes resulting in patchy, irregular supervision of the operation.

To achieve satisfactory performance from the sealant the joint groove should be absolutely dry and absolutely clean otherwise poor adhesion of the sealant to the groove walls will result. Within reason the groove walls should be square. An irregular groove will result in poor joint performance. It is usually more advisable to cut back to sound material to achieve a regular if somewhat over-wide joint than to attempt to reform the joint groove to the specified dimension by patching with a chemical mortar.

Check that the joint groove is to the specified depth, too deep a groove may result in the sealer 'hanging up' on the groove side whereas too shallow a groove may result in the sealer pulling out of the groove through insufficient adhesion to the groove walls.

Oversize joints are, of course, wasteful of joint sealer which is an expensive material.

The joint sealer in expansion joints should well fill the groove otherwise stones may wedge in the gap, jamming the joint and damaging its edges.

Coupled with the requirements for cleanliness and dryness is the equally vital necessity, with hot run sealants, of checking that the joint sealer is heated to and poured at the temperature stipulated by the manufacturer. This necessitates constant monitoring, the most common fault being overheating of the sealer in antiquated melters fitted with broken or inaccurate thermometers.

Cold applied or preformed sealers avoid the difficulties sometimes encountered in using hot run sealers but otherwise they require equally careful attention.

Kerbs and paving slabs

Sweetness of line on a radius is the ultimate judge of a kerb line, and if this is achieved the rest of the kerbing is usually satisfactory. Straight line and level can be set by instrument, and radii by radius pegs, but the final outcome lies in the hands of the kerb layer, a good one can be very good requiring little, if any, correction. All his work though will be as nought if the bedding and haunching to the kerb is weak. The kerb line and level determines the road line and level and so supervision of the kerbs' firmness in place should be strict. Kerbs are very vulnerable to damage from construction traffic and should be checked immediately prior to and during the different courses of road construction.

67

Regularity and evenness of joint lines and firmness of bedding are the requirements for good paving, the first two can be judged by eye and the third by walking over the slabs. Pay attention to falls, especially at intersections where areas of different fall meet.

Masonry

Stone masonry blockwork is not much used nowadays. Where it is, the normal principles of blockwork need to be observed, *viz* bedding, jointing, bonding.

Masonry facework again follows these principles, together with a requirement to be tied securely to the structure which supports it. The blocks, being facework, should be in first class condition.

Mechanical and electrical installations

Most projects include the installation of mechanical and electrical plant to a greater or lesser extent so brief mention will be made here of some of the more important considerations of this extensive subject.

Plant is usually expensive and of long delivery so ensure that it is stored safely when on site. Once it is installed, see that it is protected from the building work which will very probably still be progressing around it, plastering for instance or floor screeds around the machinery plinths.

Plant installation may require a cleaner environment than concurrent construction activities and finer tolerances. To avoid disputes between different contractors, priorities and disciplines, careful programming is required.

Civil work precedes mechanical installation so ensure that suitable openings are provided for plant accommodation. Avoid the classic mistake of completing a building without leaving sufficient access for the entry of machinery. With small openings, pipe and cable penetrations, for example, or small air conditioning ductwork, it may be more convenient to build first and cut out later. Records of all such builder's work should be agreed between Contractor and Inspector.

The most common building involvements with plant installations are the provision of machinery plinths and the grouting up or dry packing required under machinery base plates and holding down bolts. Running grout into pockets for the purpose of securing holding down bolts is a fairly straightforward exercise, but dry packing mortar under machinery base plates requires more attention. A common fault is to pack around the perimeter of a large base leaving the interior hollow and thus unsupported. The extent of the packing and its soundness are items for inspection, as too are the mixes used both for grout and dry pack.

Electrical cable seems to be particularly prone to damage after it has been installed or laid. If damage occurs the cable run will need complete replacement if joints are inadmissible.

Paints and painting

Protective painting, as opposed to decorative painting, is one of those activities which goes on and on and tends to be overlooked in the general hustle of site work.

Determined inspection is required and this usually includes awkward clambers up ladders and along scaffolding to reach roof beams, columns and other high level work.

No matter how sophisticated the paint system specified it will not last long if the base to which it is applied is badly prepared, so first and above all ensure that preparation is thoroughly executed. The successive coats which then follow are usually of different colours, deliberately, to enable a check to be made that each has been applied and that coverage of the individual layers is complete.

A check should be made on the consistency of the paint and the film thicknesses. Cans of thinners on site, ostensibly used for cleaning brushes and equipment, should be viewed with suspicion. Drums of paint should be identified before the manufacturers' markings are obliterated by paint runs, if this is not done there is no ready way of identifying otherwise anonymous paint drums in use. Check that the pot life or shelf life of the paint has not been exceeded.

Piling

In this section sheet piles, driven bearing piles and *in-situ* piles are considered.

Steel sheet piling should be checked regularly during driving for plumb and for progression, eg the tendency to creep in the line the piling is progressing. Check that the correct type and length of pile is being used and that the piles are driven to their correct depth.

Inspect the condition of the clutches, a damaged clutch will hinder pitching and driving and reduce the water tightness and strength of the connection.

Where special piles are made up to fill gaps or for junctions, check their fabrication for strength of weld, bolting, rivetting or other fastenings.

Steel bearing piles are wellnigh indestructable. If they need to be extended in length ensure that a strong weld has been made and any end damage cut off before welding on the new section.

Precast concrete bearing piles should be carefully checked for damage, especially for cracks which may be very fine, at all stages from the casting yard to the final set in place. Even the strongest of such piles is susceptible to damage in handling, quite apart from any damage which may arise during driving.

Driven bearing piles should be checked for set and length of penetration.

There are many variations of the cast *in-situ* pile and diameters range up to 1 m and more. The aim is to achieve a sound pillar of concrete in the ground with the reinforcement correctly placed and no inclusions of earth in the concrete. In some instances with lined piles it is possible to inspect the ground at the foot of the pile and the condition of any belled out ends if required. Samples of the soil passed through should be taken for analysis whilst the pile is being sunk.

The as-constructed position of piles or pile groups should be surveyed and compared with the details shown on the drawings. The presence of out of tolerance piles may necessitate a new design for the pile cap or may even require further pile(s) to be provided.

Bored vertical piles should be plumbed to check their depth whilst their verticality can be checked by means of a light suspended down the bore.

Plasters, renders and screeds

Simply, though skilfully applied, these items require attention at joints. Joints in the underlying structure should not be simply covered over or unsightly sympathetic surface cracks will develop. Where screeds are laid to fall, check that the falls are correct and that the specified thicknesses are achieved, too thin a screed will soon break up. Laying screeds around machinery plinths is awkward work which should be checked to avoid backfalls or flat spots. If lightweight screed is used, check practically that it is lightweight and not just a weak mortar or concrete mix.

Certain screeds require to be laid monolithically with the underlying slab, others are cast separately, check that the correct method is used.

Precast construction

Of prime importance in precast construction are setting out and joint construction, neither leaves much room for error.

Because precast items, by definition, come ready made there is little tolerance for errors in setting out. If, to correct error, specials are required to be cast, and cured, a delay in erection will probably ensue. So ensure that setting out is accurately done to line, level, plumb and square.

The correct making of joints is vital to the stability of precast erection whether the joints be wet or dry, ie cast in or mechanically fastened, and every joint should be inspected individually. Where mechanical fastenings are used check that the fastenings themselves are securely anchored.

During erection check that stability is maintained at all times by adequate temporary support. Precast items can be heavy and awkward to handle and are not necessarily self-stable.

Inspect all items for damage before, during and after erection, careless handling or stacking can crack a precast item quite easily.

Precast yard

The precast yard on site will be set up with repetition very much in mind and will resemble the yard of a precast components manufacturer. A large yard should have its own batching plant and cranage facilities. Precast production is run to a tight schedule so it is necessary for the yard to be self-sufficient regarding production facilities.

Note the extent, level and soundness of the base slab. Precast units will almost certainly be built to fine tolerances of dimension and finish, requiring firmly founded shutters. The shutters themselves, probably of steel, should be strong enough for repetitive use. Check that they are not damaged.

Curing arrangements should be extensive, preferably with a piped water supply or other purpose-built arrangement. Arrangements for handling and stacking units should be adequate for the yard's production. This is an important consideration if excessive and expensive wastage, caused by units broken during handling and stacking, is to be avoided. Remember that a delay in construction may ensue if replacement units have to be cast and cured to achieve completion. It is normal to cast spare units to guard against such an eventuality and it is wise to check that this is in fact being done.

Lighting arrangements should be generous, especially over the casting beds for safety's sake and to assist inspection. Insist on improvement if the lighting is poor.

Good organisation is essential for a well-run yard, not only for reasons of logistics but also to keep track of the often hundreds of identical items being manufactured. Both Contractor and Inspector should keep comprehensive records of the day-by-day casting of items and their scheduled curing and stacking times, otherwise below strength items may erroneously and perhaps disasterously be used in the works. All items should be referenced and date-marked on casting.

Pressure grouting

Pressure grouting can be a very simple or a very complex operation, utilising at one extreme simple pumps and cement grout and at the other sophisticated pumps and complex chemical grouts. Here only the former is considered though certain basic principles apply to both.

First and foremost it is the machinery which should be checked, the mixer, the pump, and perhaps above all, the pressure gauges (more than one is desirable). Mixers and pumps are robust and well understood on site, but pressure gauges are neither. Check the condition and calibration of the gauges and have them identical if possible. The attitude that any old pair of gauges is satisfactory is neither acceptable nor safe. Too low a pressure will result in unsound grouting, too high a pressure may well cause serious damage to the works.

The grout itself should be checked for composition and for the volume used. Where possible, estimate beforehand how much grout is expected to be used. This is straightforward enough when deliberately formed holes are being filled, but can only be very approximate, if, say, grouting under slabs or into ground is in operation. Check tell-tales and elsewhere for signs of grout as the operation proceeds.

Reinforcement
Starting from scratch, the only way to check reinforcement is to take the drawing out on site and check bar for bar. Usually the standard of bar fixing is quite good, making checking fairly straightforward.

Reinforcement should be checked to see that the correct type and size of bar is used, that the bars are at the correct centres and correctly located in the shutters. Measure lap lengths and ensure that correct cover has been provided, top, bottom and side, as appropriate. The bars should be free from oil, grease, excessive rust, mortar runs from previous pours, and should be securely fixed. If the bars project a distance beyond the shutters, temporary support may be required. If the reinforcement has been pre-assembled in cages check that temporary welding has not damaged the permanent reinforcement.

The wires should not touch the shutter sides. If they do they will cause rust marks on the concrete face. For the same reason all loose wire should be cleared from the shutters before casting.

Look for the pattern of reinforcement appropriate to the section under inspection. Beams, columns, slabs, cantilevers, retaining walls etc, each have their own typical reinforcement pattern and knowing this facilitates checking. Look for regularity and note any gaps.

Retaining walls
These structures come in a variety of forms ranging from simple vertical cantilevers to high counterforted walls. Construction should recognise the principles on which the design is based. The main reinforcement in a simple reinforced concrete retaining wall will run vertically but check that it is in the correct face of the wall. The main reinforcement in the slab of a counterforted retaining wall will run horizontally but again check that it is in the correct face of the slab and check that the reinforcement in the counterforts is all present and correctly positioned. Where the drawings show successive reductions in the amount of reinforcement, ensure that the correct reinforcement is provided to at least the minimum positions required

in each face and in each direction. Ensure that weepholes or other drainage facilities are maintained both during and after construction.

Roofing and flooring

Where prefabricated units are used to form roofing or flooring, attention should be paid to their all round stability during all stages of construction. Check that the units cannot slip off their bearings and, if the units are used compositely with *in-situ* concrete, see if they form a self-supporting working platform or if propping is necessary. Metal decking is particularly vulnerable to deflection when being worked on.

Roofing is usually required to provide occasional light access only, so prevent excessive or careless access during laying or accidents and damaged sheets may be the result.

Close attention to the laying, lapping, jointing, and finishing of waterproofing membranes is essential and again access should be restricted to prevent damage.

Secondary steelwork

Chapter 6, Structural Steelwork covers all the major aspects of steelwork construction. Apart from structural work a good deal of steelwork in one form or another is usually present on a project, as for example in miscellaneous framing, floor supports, staircases and cladding supports. However, the observations made regarding good practice in structural work apply equally to secondary items.

Supervision of this work should concentrate on observing that fixings are well made, alignments correct and protective treatments undamaged. Without these, unsatisfactory line or level to finished work will result and with secondary steelwork being of lighter section, corrosion may turn into a major nuisance and expense. Where steelwork is used to form the support to mechanical or electrical plant items, ensure that the foundations are firm and level and the framing securely braced.

Services (buried)

Where no services exist beforehand, the installation of buried services is saved the complication, extreme at times, of having to avoid them. The installation of buried services, even in a clear field, is not without complications though where interests conflict.

See that services are installed at their specified depths, levels and falls, and that accurate records are kept of fixings, fittings and any departures from the lines shown on the working drawings.

Correct backfilling to trenches is important, especially across areas to be surfaced later. Backfilling around and between adjacent services is equally important. It is normal procedure to compact ground first and then excavate to lay services, otherwise the compacting plant may damage the services if these are laid beforehand. Ensure too that all buried services are installed, or provided for, before surfacing commences or many will be the recriminations.

Cable ducts and other buried pipework should be sealed temporarily to prevent blockage during backfilling. Manholes and draw pits should be similarly treated. Note that buried services are more vulnerable to damage during and after laying than when overlying construction is complete, so ensure that they are adequately protected, and marked, at all times.

Check that draw wires have been provided in cable ducts.

Where the presence of existing services is known, if not their number or whereabouts, try to obtain local information but do not be surprised or disappointed if this is less than comprehensive. Quite often it is only during the laying of new services that existing services can be located and recorded, or even their presence discovered. Identifying existing services once found presents further problems — pipes in the ground can look all very much the same. Cables are particularly awkward to deal with in that they are hard to identify if old, even though diverting may be a simple operation. Most local authorities are prompt in assisting in the diversion of their existing services. Note that diverting and rejointing major telephone cables is a lengthy procedure.

Services (mounted)

The installation of mounted services, eg cables, air conditioning ducts, general plumbing and lightning protection, is usually fairly straightforward. Apart from technical correctness the services should be mounted neatly and regularly for the sake of appearance, especially if surface mounted, and ease of maintenance. Check that all colour coding and other identification systems are correctly executed and recorded.

Many services will require lagging, often to a detailed specification, so check that the correct materials and thicknesses are applied and that joints and laps are soundly made. Pay particular attention to corners, junctions, valves and other fittings, especially if the original lagging has to be disturbed.

Expansion joints in services and their coverings should match the expansion joints in the supporting structure.

Setting out

Setting out (as opposed to surveying), so important to get right and often having serious consequences if wrong, is usually entrusted to junior members of staff. Responsibility for the correctness of setting out normally rests with the Contractor, but the Inspector cannot escape some share of the blame, even if only morally, if a mistake is made.

Setting out is not a text book exercise of marking line or measuring level but a practical activity of establishing in the field lines and levels shown on drawings. Some advice is given below:

1 Check setting out independently wherever possible.
2 Ensure that field datums are backed up by primary and secondary datums so that if disturbed, as they most certainly will be, they can be re-established accurately.
3 Mark all datums boldly and see that they are protected.
4 Double check negative levels, ie those below zero site datum, and the relative effect on established levels if datum levels are adjusted.
5 Modern surveying instruments enable fast, accurate work to be done but the simple plumb bob and carpenter's level still have their uses.
6 When setting out work, establish offset lines or lines clear of the work otherwise the lines will be lost when construction starts.
7 Assistance is usually hard to find.
8 Check all instruments and tapes before commencing work.

Slabs
Slabs made from prefabricated units may need stabilising temporarily in their uncompleted state. Bearing areas should be sound and level throughout.

Stairs
The setting up of stairs for casting on site always seems to give rise to unnecessary concern, and the practical co-ordination of top and bottom supports with goings, risings, and waist thickness is best left to the carpenters erecting the shuttering. It is important to check that the waist thickness remains constant, whilst maintaining the designed thickness, and that correct allowance has been made for finishes on slabs, landings, and on the stairs themselves.

Tanking and waterproofing
Continuity is an essential requirement in the application of these materials so pay close attention to all laps, joints, and other locations where sheets or painted coatings overlap. Corners are vulnerable, particularly the base/wall corner which is often the most awkward to inspect.

The surfaces to which the water proofing is being applied should be smooth and without projections which may easily puncture the waterproofing.

A common trouble area is where the waterproofing crosses construction joints in the surfaces to be covered where the surface finish is often rougher than the adjacent surfaces. Back filling against an externally waterproofed structure may also cause damage to the waterproofing.

If a painted coating is being applied, ensure that the painting is liberal and thorough, filling surface indentations, and that the correct number of coats is provided.

Timber components

Structural timber units, like other prefabricated structural units, require careful handling and stacking on site and in the yard. Inspection should concentrate on the state of repair of the units and the condition of the timber itself.

Structural timber components rely not only on the intrinsic strength of the timber, but also on the strength and efficiency of their joints and connections. Careful inspection of all these items is necessary.

Supervision of erection should follow usual principles with particular attention being paid to bearings, stability and handling.

Water bar

There is a strong school of thought which considers water bars to be more trouble than they are worth. Be that as it may, water bars are in widespread use at joints in water retaining/excluding structures and, properly fixed, are effective in helping to ensure watertight joints, though an otherwise badly made joint will not be made watertight simply by the presence of a water bar. The majority of water bars in use are manufactured in rubber or plastic compositions and these are the kinds now considered.

Water bars should be fixed tautly and securely in the shutters. Where eyelets are present, they should be used tidily, care being taken not to tear the water bar material. During concreting, great care should be taken in placing and vibrating the concrete adjacent to the water bar to ensure thorough compaction without damage to the water bar. Where the water bar passes through the shutter, the joint should be sealed as tightly as possible to prevent grout loss. Honeycombing against a water stopped joint defeats the object and cutting out or patching up the defective concrete only makes matters worse. The water bar/shutter joint is the most critical one to inspect and needs thorough checking.

The water bar itself should be checked for physical damage, ie splits or tears, and to see if it has deteriorated at all during storage. Joints should be carefully checked, whether site or factory made. Concrete droppings and any deleterious material, such as grease, oil or shutter oil, should be cleaned off before concreting begins.

It is also important to check that the water bar is safe from damage where it projects outside the shutters.

Check that the right type of water bar is being used and that it is correctly positioned in the shutter.

5 Stages of Construction

The purpose of this chapter is to describe the progress of a typical medium to large construction project from its very beginning to its completion, and to consider the varying needs and levels of supervision as the work proceeds. The progress of a project may be considered as falling into three stages – the beginning, the middle and the end, but here it is discussed as though there were five stages, these being colloquially:

1 Possession of the site
2 Starting up
3 Full swing construction
4 Running down and completion
5 Maintenance period

This five stage sequence is followed generally throughout this chapter, though the section boundaries are not distinct. The pattern of progress is common to projects large or small; they all have a beginning, a middle and an end. Each stage has characteristics of its own and supervision needs to be flexible in order to adjust to the changing requirements.

The early stages of a contract are arguably the most interesting with the setting up of offices and workshops, the arrival of plant and materials, the studying of the drawings and general sizing up of the work to be done. Procedures and organisation worked out now can affect, beneficially or adversely, the progress of the job in its later stages.

During its middle period a project should run itself, meaning that by this time procedures are established and understood by all, and a working routine progresses in all parts of the site. The pressure of work can be considerable, even if a bit repetitive, and then suddenly, almost overnight, it is finished, and only finishing off remains.

The closing stage is one of repeated inspection and the making of lists of items requiring attention or finishing. The contents of the lists will progress with time from the general to the particular to the individual until all items are complete. In this stage the focus is on administration rather than construction, to see a tidy end to the project.

If at all possible it is preferable for staff to see a project through from start to finish. Continuity and knowledge of the job is invaluable when the time comes for answering measurement queries, adjusting claims and the compilation of records, quite apart from the

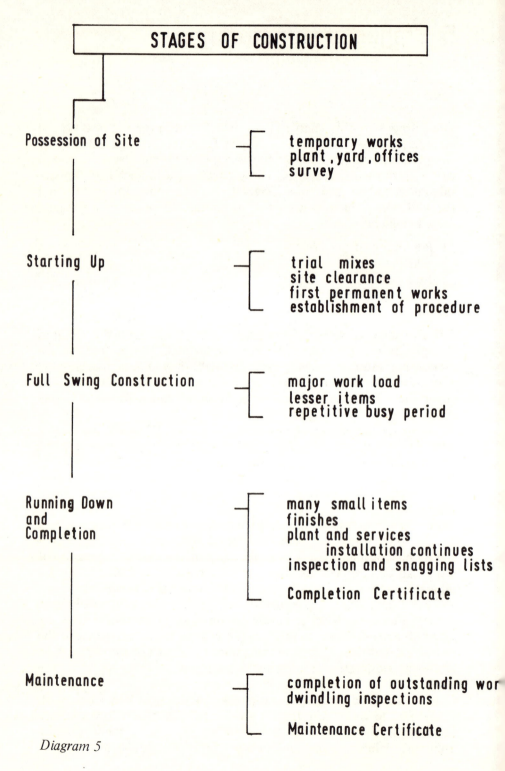

STAGES OF CONSTRUCTION

Possession of Site
- temporary works
- plant, yard, offices
- survey

Starting Up
- trial mixes
- site clearance
- first permanent works
- establishment of procedure

Full Swing Construction
- major work load
- lesser items
- repetitive busy period

Running Down and Completion
- many small items
- finishes
- plant and services installation continues
- inspection and snagging lists

  Completion Certificate

Maintenance
- completion of outstanding wor
- dwindling inspections

  Maintenance Certificate

Diagram 5

78

personal satisfaction achieved in seeing a job through. Commonly, however, senior staff are transferred to other postings, leaving middle level and junior grades to finish off. It is a feature common to construction projects that, starting from nothing, resources of men and materials are marshalled into building the works and then, on completion, all are disbanded, leaving the works in the hands of their owner.

1 Possession of site

The Contractor will usually be first on site, establishing a temporary office for himself and one for the Inspector pending his completion of the permanent offices for both. He will also start setting up his stores and other facilities such as carpenters' shop, plant yard, steel yard, batching plant, and laboratories.

Inspection of the Contractor's activities should be commenced as soon as possible and records begun noting such significant items as the date on which the Contractor took possession of the site, the initial condition of the site and the dates of arrival of major items of plant and materials. Ideally, the Contractor should have clear and unobstructed site possession. If circumstances obtain that prevent this, then the causes should be noted and jointly agreed between the Contractor and Inspector. It is advantageous to take photographs at this stage of the condition of the site and of whatever happens to be on it.

On a major contract of, say, four years' duration it may well be that the first year is spent in setting up site and constructing temporary works, site access, camps and the like. This is especially so where seasonal working is necessitated by, for example, river flows or severe weather conditions.

Temporary works may be, in themselves, quite substantial undertakings whose satisfactory performance may be important to the successful and timely completion of a project. Attention should be paid to their construction almost equal to that paid to the permanent works. The diversion of a river by temporary channels or banks, the construction of a haulroad for quarried materials or a bridge for site access are examples of major temporary works which should not be left unchecked during or after construction. Perhaps contrary to popular practice, the Inspector should concern himself with these undertakings, because, apart from the need to be assured that the works are fit enough for the job they have to do, the way the Contractor sets about them both in planning and execution can be a useful guide to his attitude to the permanent works.

Plant when it arrives on site may or may not be in a fit working condition. If it has come direct from a previous site it may be, if it comes from a plant depot it should be. Make a note of the major items and their condition as they arrive. If key items are late or unserviceable, substitutes may be reqiured which could be a problem on remote sites.

One of the very first requirements after possession of the site will be the need to secure the site with temporary, or permanent, fencing. The importance of this is three-fold; firstly to prevent unauthorised access and achieve internal security; secondly to guard against the possibility of injury to third parties who might otherwise unwittingly enter the site; and thirdly to provide a replacement for any existing property boundary fencing on land on which the contract encroaches. Landowners the world over are extremely sensitive to any changes in their property boundaries and they will not be the least of a project's problems if their demands or complaints are not paid due regard.

Both Contractor and Inspector will want to make a thorough inspection of the site as soon as possible, apart from the survey undertaken at first possession, probably both jointly and separately. On a self-contained project this may not take more than a few hours, but on a 'ribbon' contract, as for say a motorway, canal or pipe line, it may take several days, with access and distance being the time consuming elements. The detail of inspection will vary inversely with the speed of travel. An inspection on foot will reveal more detail than one by car, though the rate of progress will naturally be slower. Unusual these days, but most effective on certain projects, is an inspection on horseback which combines the advantages of mobility, a good vantage point, and ability to cover a fair distance. On inspections, look out for features which may need special consideration and note them carefully. They should be, but may not be, shown on the contract drawings, depending on the accuracy of the original site survey. It is never possible to show all minor topographical features. Conversely, those features which are shown on the drawings should be identified and evaluated.

Together with the site inspection will be the requirement for an accurate site level grid to establish and record existing ground levels. This survey will be undertaken and agreed jointly by Contractor and Inspector. The size of grid on which the levels are taken will depend on the terrain being covered, irregular terrain requiring a closely spaced grid whilst a level terrain can be covered by a wide grid. The contract drawings do not usually show existing levels in sufficient detail to be used for accurate measurement purposes. The level survey will pick up all topographical features and provide a useful back-up to the contract layout drawings.

Concurrent with the site survey will be the establishment of line and level datums at convenient locations throughout the site to enable detailed setting out of the permanent works to proceed. These datums should preferably be established jointly and should certainly be checked for correctness before permanent work commences. Mistakes have an unfortunate habit of compounding, affecting not only the immediate structure but adjacent ones too, particularly connecting services. So, quite apart from any contractual obligations, master datums should be checked and double checked for everyone's peace of mind.

2 Starting up

Following the completion of the site level survey, site clearance will commence. This may be regar ed as the commencement of work proper clearing the way as it does for excavation, filling and the opening up of foundations.

Top soil should be stripped and stockpiled separately from other fill and, to avoid confusion, it is wise to record the positions of top soil tips on drawings. Other soil, if suitable and required for construction, will be run to stockpile or laid as fill whilst unsuitable soil will be run to tip off site. It is important to check that the top soil has been properly stripped to an adequate depth and also that depressions are not buried in loose fill during the general clearance operations. If there are buildings to be demolished they should be photographed first for record purposes. Basements, cellars, septic tanks and other buried structures need not necessarily be completely demolished but may be cut down to an agreed level and backfilled carefully. The diversion of existing services will probably be scheduled during this period and the site clearance operations could well reveal the presence of previously unplotted services also requiring diversion. It is also prudent to photograph or survey, if permissible, existing property adjacent to the site which might possibly be adversely affected by construction activities. Vibration, noise and dust all have nuisance values which may give rise to grounds for claims for damage.

Access to different parts of the site may be difficult at this time whilst the site roads are being established and gaining access to the more remote parts of the site can become a hard, time-consuming slog. It is, however, most important to keep in constant contact with all areas of work right from the start, and repeated journeys do have the merit of acquainting one early with the site geography, landmarks, and ground conditions.

Where contracts are let in sections as, for example, in motorway construction, it is important that common line and level datums are co-ordinated at the section interfaces. The need to establish the common centre line speaks for itself, if only to avoid the railway line cartoon situation. Level datums are necessary for, amongst other reasons, grade and drainage connections. The co-ordination of service runs, and perhaps even the materials used in construction will also be necessary. These may seem obvious points to make but they are too easily put off from day to day for reasons of other pressing business, remoteness of the adjoining contracts and awkwardness in communications.

3 Full swing construction

With the completion of site clearance and the opening of foundations construction momentum soon picks up and working patterns establish into full swing construction. Taking reinforced concrete construction as an example, by the time that the first structural concrete, usually a base or footing, is ready for casting, concrete mixes should have been tested and approved; indeed casting should not proceed until the relevant mix has been approved. A routine for inspection should also have been agreed, which routine may only be a preliminary one at this early stage, but at least there must be an acknowledged procedure. It might not work right the first time and misunderstandings between Contractor and Inspector are bound to occur from time to time, but procedure there should be from which a working relationship can be established.

The procedure generally follows the pattern thus:

Notification by the Contractor to the Inspector that an item is ready for casting.
Inspection by the Inspector.
Correction by the Contractor if so required by the Inspector.
Second inspection by the Inspector.
Approval by the Inspector.
Construction proceeds.

Inspections may be done jointly by the Inspector and Contractor or by the Inspector separately. It does not usually matter though on balance it is better if the Contractor is present if the workload permits. If the Contractor cannot be present, it is important that he be promptly advised of the outcome of any inspection and that any verbal instructions to him by the Inspector be given to an accredited responsible representative and not just anyone who happens to be around. Failure to observe this procedure will almost inevitably result in the Contractor insisting, quite rightly, that all further instructions be given formally in writing – a laborious and time-consuming exercise (for both parties), and one which normally doesn't survive very long, by mutual consent. The procedure may be as rigid or as relaxed as workmanship or relationships allow. Usually, to the advantage of both parties, some type of written request/comment/approval site form is introduced to allow notice to be given and inspection, comment (if any), and approval to be recorded. When supervising the work of sub-contractors it is important, always, to deal with them through the main Contractor. Instructions should never be issued direct to sub-contractors.

As the contract proceeds fresh activities get underway, sometimes it seems at an almost overwhelming rate. It is common practice to require the Contractor to prepare a Method Statement for each major activity. As its name implies, this is a statement of the Contractor's intended method of working. These statements are subject to the approval of the Inspector. Inspection procedures for each activity have to be established but, assuming that the procedure for the major base load activity is set up and working well, the procedures for supervising additional work usually follow the main pattern easily and are soon absorbed into the daily routine of site life. It will seem though, during the build up and early months of full swing construction, that this is a period when everything is starting and nothing is finishing, which of course is just what is happening and there will be no let-up for a while. The major work base load will be the first to start and the last to finish, though its character may change as sections are completed. For instance, superstructure will follow foundations, or pavement concrete will follow dry lean concrete, which follows subgrade compaction, and, superimposed from time to time on these activities will be others such as roofing, cladding, installation of machinery or the laying of services and making of joints. It has been estimated that in a bill of quantities for a construction project, twenty per cent of the items account for eighty per cent of the value of the works. It is this twenty per cent base load that, once set going, is relatively straightforward to control, whereas the remaining eighty per cent of the items are more demanding of supervision. It will soon be observed that these 'secondary' activities – secondary only by comparison – require just as much planning and a greater variety of detailed supervision than the major items. Once the initial trials are over and procedures established, the construction of heavy foundations, erection of superstructure, laying and compaction of fill or pavement laying, falls into a repetitious pattern and therein lies a danger. This danger is that the repetition of similar procedures or construction of similar units can lead to complacency, lack of diligence and so, maybe, to trouble. Close attention should be paid at all times to the interpretation of the laboratory monitoring controls and other checks which have been designed and set up to record standards of quality and to indicate when specified standards are not being achieved. And here another danger presents itself, that of relaxing the specification in order to allow work to continue according to programme. Only after the most careful consideration should any relaxation be permitted, if at all. There may well be extenuating circumstances or precedents for a less rigid control but each individual request should be considered on its merits and the matter referred to Head Office if deemed necessary or beyond the scope of site competence/authority. Other systems of checks will have also been devised to guard against the omission of built-in items or to highlight the occurrence of specials in a run of otherwise similar sections. Examples of laboratory controls are charts for recording the strength of successive concrete test cubes or earthwork densities and percentage compaction. Examples of construction checks are special drawings produced on site to co-ordinate civil, mechanical and electrical services for each section of the works.

In contrast to the few major items which comprise the bulk of the work the 'secondary' non repetitious items usually demand constant careful supervision and a good deal of ingenuity to get the fiddly bits right.

The newcomer to a busy site may well be excused some bewilderment during his first few weeks until the pattern of operations becomes apparent. What might at first seem to be a confusion of activity resolves itself into an ordered sequence of working, much of it repetitious as explained in the foregoing paragraphs. The execution of immediate day-to-day duties will soon make familiar the details and routine of the particular section of the works to which he is assigned but as an introduction the outline sequence of operations in the construction of two common types of work are now described, these being, firstly, a simple reinforced two-storey concrete building and secondly, typical pavement construction. The procedure is described in broad terms to indicate the sequence of construction; the points to observe in the detailed supervision and inspection are described separately in chapter 4 on elements of construction. The separate chapters 6 and 7 on Earthworks and Structural Steelwork contain similar construction sequence descriptions for these two major disciplines.

Construction of a typical two storey concrete framed building
After the completion of site clearance and removal of top soil, preliminary setting out for foundation excavation will be required. The setting out will involve the establishment of longitudinal and transverse centre lines and bench marks for a working level reference. Excavation may comprise mass excavation if the structure is founded generally below existing ground level, trenches for strip footings or independent bases for columns. The latter is the example being taken here. Once preliminary excavation is complete, levels are again established by pegs set to the level of the top of the blinding and the excavation trimmed to level and the blinding cast. Accurate centre lines and other lines and levels will now be required for the erection to line and level of shutters, which is followed by the fixing of base reinforcement and any starter bars necessary for ground beams and columns. The base is then cast, care being taken not to displace or damage the shutters and reinforcement. After the required interval the base shutters are struck and the reinforcement for the columns fixed again, not forgetting any starter bars, followed by erection of the column shutters. The shutters should be checked for line, plumb, storey height, cover to reinforcement, strength and bracing, all as previously described before, during and after casting. After the

required interval the column shutters may be struck carefully to avoid damage to faces and corners. A newly cast column is vulnerable to site damage and should be protected, in fact columns are always vulnerable and should always be protected, especially from vehicles during the construction period. Dumpers are a particular menace in this respect and so, later, will be the vehicles bringing and compacting fill within and around the building.

Following completion of the columns, scaffolding is erected to support the first floor shutters for beams and slab. The scaffolding will normally be founded on the natural ground or on a blinding layer rather than on any compacted fill which may be required to bring the ground level to underside of ground floor slab, due to risk of settlement.

A level datum will be required on the columns to set the first floor shutters, soffit and edge, to level and setting-out lines needed for edge and beam shutters. Reinforcement is then fixed for beams and slab, any built-in items secured and the concrete cast. During casting a check should be made on the security of the supporting scaffolding and shutters, also that the correct thickness of slab is maintained throughout, not just at the edges where the perimeter shutters provide the guide. A similar routine is followed for the second lift of columns and for the roof slab and beams. In this case scaffolding is supported off the first floor which must itself remain propped until the roof slab is self supporting.

After the formwork and scaffolding have been removed, fill will be brought up to level within the building, blinding laid, reinforcement fixed and the ground slab cast. Prior to this any buried services will have been installed with suitable provision in the slab for final connections.

During the construction period, and apart from the items noted above, checks will also have been made on the following aspects; the condition and strength of the soil beneath the column bases, samples of the concrete used in the various pours, supervision of all concrete pours, thoroughness of the curing measures, compaction of backfill to the ground slabs.

A typical concrete pavement construction
In pavement construction site clearance and top soil stripping are followed by excavation or fill to the required formation level, line and level being controlled by profiles or pegs arranged at regular, convenient intervals throughout the site.

The specification may require the soil below formation level to be compacted to a stated value in which case, where excavation to reach formation is required, the soil may be removed to below formation level and then relaid in the specified controlled manner to achieve the required strength. Where fill to formation level is required, the stripped ground surface will be levelled, bad areas removed and refilled with approved material and the whole area compacted prior to the commencement of the fill. Fill will then be brought up to the required formation level in an approved manner. The approved manner will have been resolved in compaction trials held prior to the commencement of earthworks. Subgrade compaction and/or compaction of fill to formation level is vitally important no matter how strong or comprehensive the specified successive superimposed layers of pavement construction may be. A failure in the underlying soil will soon be reflected by surface failure.

The early stages of pavement construction are ones of earthworks, soil sampling and testing, cut or fill, compaction and density measurement, a continuous demand for control of setting out, line and level.

Items such as drainage culverts, services, cable ducts and other buried crossings should now be constructed, ie before commencement of the pavement layers begins but, generally and depending of course on their relative levels, after the completion of earthworks' compaction. Their construction will follow the normal pattern for such items. Special care should be taken to ensure that the full required thickness of overlying construction, pavement or fill, is available above them when completed. Check too that the items extend sufficiently clear beyond the pavement and shoulder edges, not forgetting any allowance for slopes, drainage ditches, etc. Any structures such as manholes, draw pits, valve pits and floodlight bases, located within the pavement and finished flush with its surface, require careful checking for level. The compaction of backfill around all structures and services should be most carefully controlled.

The laying of the several layers, which together form the pavement construction proper, now follows in an orderly and repetitious sequence, the routine of construction being similar whichever materials are chosen. As with earthworks, the various pavement layers will be laid and compacted in methods approved in previous trials. Within the separate divisions of concrete or bituminous construction some choice is usually left to the Contractor regarding the use of alternative materials, subject to approval by the Inspector. A motorway utilising bituminous surfacing may, for example, be built up as follows:

The subgrade, ie the soil to formation level.
The sub-base of graded stone.
The roadbase of a cement bound material.
The base course of a bituminous material.
The wearing course of a bituminous material.

Each of these layers will require checking for level and the quality of its constituents, the tolerances becoming tighter for each superimposed layer. The top three layers in the above example will be laid by paver, so staggering of joints, trimming of joints, smoothness over joints, surface planeness, tolerances and layer thicknesses all require checking for each layer.

The control of line and level and layer thickness is an unending activity whilst construction lasts whether the pavement be for an airport apron or runway, motorway or road, and this requirement may take up as much time as the other supervisory duties.

Concrete pavement construction as described earlier in chapter 4 on Elements of Construction, page 60, also involves the setting up and checking of joints of various types and the fixing of reinforcement, all sufficiently in advance to allow construction to proceed smoothly. Mass concrete slabs are sometimes used in contrast to reinforced concrete construction.

Lastly, curing and joint sealing follow, both requiring constant patient supervision. A check should be made on the restrictions on traffic movements on newly laid material and also on the time restrictions regarding the laying of successive adjacent lanes.

Laboratory quality control will have been proceeding apace with construction, sampling and testing soil characteristics, compaction, densities, gradings, constituents and strengths appertaining to the various materials in the separate layers of construction. Construction of a layer will not normally be permitted until the underlying layer has been approved in all respects.

It is hoped that these two examples have given an indication of the pattern construction takes. It is usually logical and repetitive and once the parameters of both design and construction are known and appreciated, control should be straightforward and will certainly be better than if attempted without such knowledge.

Design and construction each have their own parameters for particular types of work, the former discipline being imposed in the design office and the latter in the field. Each should be aware of the other and take cognisance of the other when works are planned, designed and executed. The maxim for good supervision could well be 'know the principle, look for the pattern'.

The documents

The drawings and the specifications are the two most obvious documents through which construction quality is controlled but two other equally important documents are the programme and the bill of quantities. As their titles indicate the purpose of these four separate documents are, respectively, to describe the extent and form of the works; to specify the contents thereof; to forecast the rate, order and time taken for construction; and to measure the quantity of work executed. Although a knowledge of the drawings and specifications is essential in the practical business of construction supervision, a working acquaintance with the programme and the bills of quantities is also necessary because, without these, anticipation of events, and hence preparation, cannot be efficient. Supervision is not just looking at the work as it happens, it is also a knowledge of what went before and what is likely to happen next.

Drawings

Drawings, specifications, programme and bills of quantities will each now be briefly discussed.

Without the drawings, work cannot start or progress, whereas without a specification, programme or bills, construction is conceivable. Though to doubtful standards, construction would nevertheless be possible.

The drawings describe on paper what is required to be built. To a non-technical person it is perhaps difficult to visualise how, say, a power station or a dock can be represented on paper in sufficient detail to enable one or the other to be built. Through experience, techniques and conventions have been developed regarding the most convenient layouts, scales and arrangement to best present the many different types of construction. It will be the first duty of site supervisory staff to study in general, and in detail, the drawings for the work in hand.

Whilst so doing it will be appreciated that the drawings for any particular section must be read together as a whole and not just one by one with no regard for adjoining drawings or different disciplines. A collage of drawings pieced together is a useful technique in gaining an overall view of the section. The project having been 'dismembered' into drawing-size pieces must now be reassembled as a whole and so studied.

The drawings should be studied not only in detail for the normal day-to-day supervision of construction, but also in more general terms in order to become familiar with the work to come next week, next month and next year. A useful exercise is to pull out all the drawings describing work past, present and future and study them together. Lessons and experience gained in the earlier stages may then be more readily appreciated and applied to future work.

Specifications

A good well written specification should be more than a dry list of standards to be met — though it will be failing in its function if it does not thoroughly and comprehensively specify the works — it should be an informative and useful guide to the good practices required in all aspects of the work for which it is written. In supervision, although personal experience counts for a great deal, such is the range of construction materials and procedures that experience cannot be expected to have met them all and experience should, in any case, always be subject to the formal requirements of the specification. The specification should be closely studied in the first place to determine the particular standards required and to ascertain if any particular method of working, sequence or restriction is to be imposed, however familiar the operation in question might be. In order to interpret correctly the meaning of some clauses it may be necessary to read them several times over where the style or convention of working is unfamiliar. As a separate exercise, and however daunting a task it might at first seem, time should be found to browse through the complete specification. It need not be a word by word study, a general knowledge of the content and scope of the specification will be invaluable in gaining an appreciation of the scope of the works as a whole. Secondly, when an operation is unfamiliar, the specification should be studied for guidance regarding criteria to observe and recommended good practice, a specification being essentially the results of the sum of experience in experiment and practice.

Programmes
Often late in being presented and received with cynicism when it appears, the Contractor's programme is nevertheless an important document in many respects, not least in enabling the arrangement of supervision to be reviewed against the forecast work load of construction.

There will be many programmes, ranging from perhaps a complex master programme so detailed that it needs a full-time operator to manage and more a record of events than a forecast of them, to a simple exercise book page bar chart for a section of the works. It is said, with a good deal of truth, that the only people who understand a programme are those who draw it, so the lesson here is to draw a programme, however simple, for each particular section of the works, and see how it compares with the official one. Preparing a short check programme entails a study of the drawings, an estimate of quantities, assessing rates of working and co-ordinating these figures with a time interval. In so doing an appreciation of the work will be gained.

The programme will be the co-ordinating tool common to all sections of the work and each section will have its own sub-programme. In a major project involving different contractors of many disciplines a programme is essential in co-ordinating their start or entry points and needs firm control if disputes are to be avoided or at least minimised. It is important to remember that a programme is not a static picture, it is bound to change frequently to reflect and forecast progress of the works, and will never be correct until the job is finished. In checking a programme, besides making a separate assessment of the quantities and work rates involved, check too the beginning and end dates, and fix or check any other key dates, and if all items and phases of work have been included in the list of activities. For example, have all separate buildings been included, has painting of steelwork been allowed for or the curing period for precast piles?

Bills of quantities
The bill of quantities — or its equivalent for assessing, measuring, listing and evaluating the items of construction — may appear an even more forbidding document than the specification.

In general supervision of construction, in the context of quality and standards control, a knowledge of the bills is not as important as a knowledge of the specification. When it comes to measurement and payment, however, it is a different matter altogether.

A study of the bills will bring an acquaintance with the quantities, materials and types of work included in the contract. It should also highlight unusual items which are not perhaps apparent on the drawings, for example special excavations, the demolition of a house or an item to be built into the works. Many bills have a preamble and this, at least, should be read.

It might be remarked that with all the documents to be studied, ie drawings, specifications, programmes and quantities it does not leave much time for the practical supervision of construction as it proceeds on site. This is fair comment but one that receives no sympathy, both should be done, with site supervision coming first. Time should also be found to at least have a glance at other sections of the works to see how they are progressing and how their progress may affect individual sections. Inspect, too, the Contractor's yard and plant workshops to gain a general impression of the stocks of materials and the state of repair, or disrepair, of plant, and assess what affect the situation may have on the progress of the works. Stocks of plaster may be running short or a vital concrete pump be broken.

4   Running down and completion
With the completion of the major works base load, the contract may be said to be beginning to run down, major work will have finished and other items will be well established. The installation of services, mechanical and electrical plant, finishes, carcassing, etc, will now occupy the majority of overseeing time. There will be a variety of smaller activities to consider rather than a comparatively few major ones. The pressure of site supervisory work will now ease, at least on the construction side if not on the services side. In contrast, the heavy administrative duties of tidily finishing off a contract will now be beginning. The ending of the major works will arrive rather abruptly, there will be little tailing off because a major works will be

attended by numerous activities necessary in full strength right to the end. For example, a bituminous paving operation takes with it pavers, rollers, lorries, the batching plant and stockpile, laboratory teams and supervisory staff right up to the last square metre. The last has to be as good as the first. The situation is similar with concrete placing or steel erection. During the course of the contract certain parts, buildings, pavements, basements, for example, will be finished before the whole and may stand unused for months prior to occupation, use, or commencement of plant installation, etc. It is bad practice to allow these parts to go unsupervised just because work is not proceeding there. They should be inspected periodically to check that they are not deteriorating through being unused or suffering in any other way. Buildings should be made secure and checked to see that they are weatherproof, settlement may have occurred or cracks or rust developed, a water mains may have become contaminated or a drain run blocked. Such temporary faults arising from neglect or oversight may have serious consequences, necessitating remedial or replacement work incurring delay or expense, probably both.

During the months prior to the completion date of the contract the contractor will be instigating the setting up and effecting of the procedures for obtaining formal contractual approval of the work he has completed. In civil engineering projects approval is normally given in the form of a completion certificate which will cover the whole of the works, or in the form of several completion certificates each of which will cover a certain area of the work as the conditions of contract may allow. Careful observation of the wording of the relevant clauses in the contract is necessary to ensure that procedure and intent are correctly observed. A detailed study of the contractual procedures followed during this period is outside the scope of this chapter which here concerns itself with the pattern of supervision on site during this phase of the contract.

The following paragraphs describe the activities which site supervision will follow, assuming the case of one completion certificate for the whole of the works.

The procedure is fundamentally one of application for a completion certificate; inspection of the complete works to check for defects and for completeness in construction and operation; correction and/or completion of the same; second inspection which if satisfactory leads to the granting of a completion certificate.

Following the signing of the completion certificate the period of maintenance begins at the expiry of which is held a further inspection to ascertain that all outstanding items have been satisfactorily finished. The maintenance certificate is then signed. One point to note is that no matter how many completion certificates there might be there is one only maintenance certificate. A proportion of the retention money is released to the Contractor at the completion certificate stage, the final proportion being released at the signing of the maintenance certificate.

In practice, several inspections will normally be required, the early ones perhaps informally recorded as being premature, and pertinent items too general for particularising, but eventually a formal inspection and list will be required, the inspections being jointly executed by representatives of the Contractor and the Inspector. Inspections should be commenced early enough to permit any major defects to be completed before the completion date, leaving only minor items outstanding. Major defects should in any case have been corrected as soon as they occurred or as soon thereafter as possible. The list, colloquially called a 'snagging list' will include all items which require correction or completion prior to the issue of a completion certificate. The list may also specifically exclude certain items, for example services and plant, which may be the subject of separate commissioning and acceptance testing, or are excluded for other valid reasons. Many construction projects include a substantial content of mechanical and electrical plant and services, examples being power stations, dry docks and steelworks. The approval of such content will be effected separately from the approval of the construction works in which they are located. Approval of such plant and services is a long and detailed procedure covering every valve, pipeline, item of machinery, etc, and may be considered as falling into two distinct phases. The first or *commissioning phase* entails starting up or putting into motion for the first time the various items involved; the second, or *acceptance phase,* entails checking the performance of the operating plant against the contract specification. Procedures separate to those for the construction work will be evolved for the approval of such items but they are eventually covered by the common maintenance certificate.

Repeated inspections will reduce the outstanding items to a few minor ones which the Contractor can undertake to complete during the maintenance period. Examples of these are such items as manhole haunchings, local making good of paintwork, replacing damaged door furniture and tidying up ditches and outfalls. At these inspections it is important to strike a reasonable commonsense balance, being neither too pernickety nor too lenient, the principle being that the Client should receive, and will be expecting to receive, a sound satisfactory project completed to accepted standards of workmanship. During this period of the contract the Contractor may be tempted to make optimistic promises in order to hasten the signing of the completion certificate. His staff, labour and plant will be running down and the Inspector should therefore take steps to ensure that the Contractor retains sufficient facilities on site to complete his obligations. The Client is normally represented at later completion inspections as well as at the maintenance inspection.

5 Maintenance period

On signing of the completion certificate, the maintenance period begins. During this period the Contractor will work off the items in the agreed list of outstanding works, at his own expense, and execute any normal wear and tear running maintenance, which may or may not be at the Client's expense.

The period is a quiet rather tedious one with inspections and approvals coming along one by one as items are completed. The Contractor will be clearing his offices and yard from site and this may include the Inspector's office and transport as well. The Contractor will also be tidying up and reinstating the site as part of his contractual obligations and it is necessary to check, and often to encourage, that all parts of the site are left in a neat and tidy state. It is also a time for the Inspector to gather up all his drawings, records, files and diaries and decide which to keep and which to discard. It is a time when Contractor's claims will be tackled and when omissions or vagueness in records will be brought to light. Site staff, leaving for other assignments, will not want to know about the job just finishing, it will be up to the few left behind to manage as best they can. When all outstanding items are complete, the Contractor and Inspector leave site. If this is prior to the actual end of maintenance arrangements are made, usually through respective Head Offices, to deal with any matters which may subsequently arise on site. A few days before the expiry of the maintenance period an inspection is held at which will be present representatives of the Contractor, the Inspector and the Client. Assuming all goes well, the maintenance certificate is then issued.

The above is a description of the usual phases of site construction, from possession of site, to starting up, full swing construction, running down, completion and finally maintenance. The phases are quite well defined and each has its own character, working methods and procedure. To be on site from start to finish is a most satisfying experience and the opportunity should be taken to do so if circumstances permit.

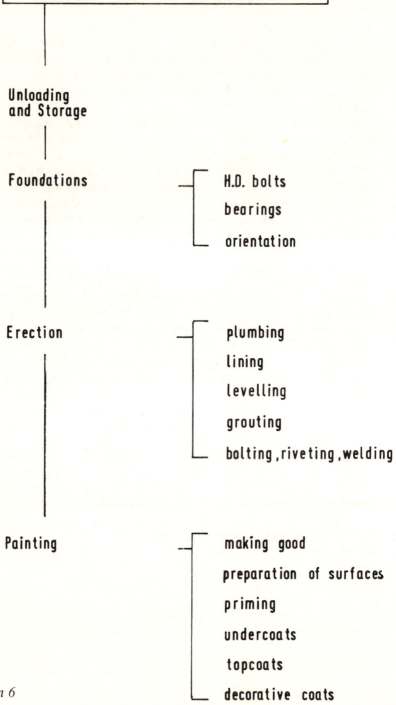

STRUCTURAL STEELWORK

Unloading
and Storage

Foundations
- H.D. bolts
- bearings
- orientation

Erection
- plumbing
- lining
- levelling
- grouting
- bolting, riveting, welding

Painting
- making good
- preparation of surfaces
- priming
- undercoats
- topcoats
- decorative coats

Diagram 6

94

6 Structural Steelwork

'Steelwork Contractor' denotes the firm commissioned to manufacture, supply and erect the structural steelwork, commonly in the capacity of sub-contractor to the general contractor.

Painting the steelwork after erection may form part of the steelwork contract, or, alternatively, a specialist firm may be employed under a separate contract. To avoid confusion, the term 'Steelwork Contractor' should be taken to mean the contractor responsible for all operations connected with the supply delivery and erection, including painting, of the structural steelwork.

This chapter is written mainly with the erection of steel framed buildings in mind, but the principles will apply in general to most other forms of steelwork construction.

Unlike *in-situ* construction, such as reinforced concrete, etc, which requires close site supervision throughout, structural steelwork comes to the site in a finished condition, ready for erection, having already been fabricated and, in the majority of cases, inspected at the fabricators' works. The duties of the Inspector will thus be directed mainly towards ensuring that the component parts of the structure are correctly placed and securely fixed in position in accordance with the working drawings, properly plumbed, lined and levelled, and finally, painted as may be specified before the structure is handed over to the other trades.

Before the erection stage is reached, however, a number of prior matters relating to the erection of the steelwork will need to be decided, amongst which may be mentioned the following:

Division of responsibility between the general contractor and the steelwork contractor for the construction of the stanchion foundations

The usual arrangements, typical of most cases, are that the general contractor is responsible for constructing the foundations and wall bearing pads, and setting holding down bolts and anchorage material in position. The HD bolts and anchorage materials are usually supplied by the steelwork contractor under the steelwork contract, and should be handed over to the general contractor in time to suit the construction programme.

The steelwork contractor is, in addition, responsible for supplying detailed information to the general contractor in the form of a foundation plan showing centres of stanchions, sizes of stanchion foundations and levels, and all relevant information regarding the

HD bolts and anchorage materials to enable these to be set correctly in position. Grouting of the stanchion base plates and girder bearings is usually undertaken by the general contractor, after plumbing, lining and levelling of the steelwork has been completed to the satisfaction of the Inspector.

The responsibility for the satisfactory completion of the erection rests, however, with the steelwork contractor, irrespective of any checking or approval of the setting-out by the general contractor or Inspector.

Erection programme

As the dates on which subsequent trades can begin their operations depends entirely upon the progress of erection of the steel framing, it is important that the sequence of erection and a time schedule for completion be drawn up and agreed to at a joint meeting of all the parties concerned, taking into account the time required for preparation and curing of the foundations and the construction of any walls on which steel beams have to rest.

Unloading and stacking areas

A suitable unloading and stacking area is required on site, on the highest ground available adjacent to the work spot, for the unloading and stacking of materials as they arrive from the fabricator's works. The area selected should be served by well consolidated access roads and an unloading apron, to prevent vehicles and cranes from being bogged down in wet weather. If the site is already served by a railway siding, as may sometimes be the case, most of these conditions will be met.

Power and water

The provision of water and electric power supply points adjacent to the work area is necessary if these are not already available on site.

Accommodation

The allocation on site of a suitable area for housing the erection site office and amenities is required, together with tools and tackle stores and paint store.

Inspection on site

To facilitate inspection the steelwork contractor should, during all working hours, have a properly accredited representitive or foreman on site together with a complete set of up-to-date contract drawings. Copies of these drawings should also be supplied to the Inspector together with any further drawings, amendments or instructions which may be issued from time to time. The drawings should include general arrangement plans of floors and roofs, drawn to a convenient scale, showing the layout of beams and stanchions with sizes and erection works, for use in marking up the progress of erection.

The Inspector should keep a daily log book for recording progress and noting any incidents or special points which may require further attention or action by the contractor(s) or Inspector. This log book will form the basis of periodical reports to be submitted to the Head Office.

Copies of delivery notes covering despatches of steelwork to the site should be furnished to the Inspector, to enable him to check that the steelwork is being delivered in time to meet the erection programme and 'chase up' any items which appear likely to cause delay.

Use of general contractor's scaffolding

Arrangements regarding the use of the general contractor's scaffolding by the steelwork contractor during the course of erection or painting of the steelwork should be decided beforehand unless the matter is specifically determined in the conditions of contract.

Service pipes and conduits

Details of any holes required in the steelwork to pass service pipes and conduits, particularly for larger diameter pipes, should be furnished to the steelwork contractor by the specialist sub-contractors concerned in good time for these holes to be provided during fabrication, otherwise costly site work may be required involving claims for additional costs. This also applies to any other specialist work which may require holes to be drilled in the steelwork, eg lift machinery, etc.

Foundations

An essential prerequisite for the smooth and accurate erection of structural steelwork is the construction of the stanchion foundations to the correct centre lines and levels, together with the accurate setting in position of the HD bolts for the stanchion base plates. These are matters to which the Inspector should give special attention.

The stanchion foundation plan to be supplied by the steelwork contractor, based on fixed grid or reference lines, should provide the general contractor with the following information:

Position of all stanchions relative to the grid lines.
Sizes and depths of foundation blocks and levels of top of concrete.
Sizes of stanchion base plates and centres of HD bolts.
Lengths and diameters of HD bolts, with details of anchorage
    materials and their location in the foundations.

97

Depth to which HD bolts are to be set in the foundation blocks to allow sufficient projection for grouting under the steel bases and for bolting the stanchion down after erection.

It is general practice to finish the top of the concrete foundation not less than 25 mm below the final underside of steel base level, to allow some latitude for minor errors in concrete levels and to facilitate the levelling and plumbing of the stanchions. The stanchion bases are wedged and packed up to the required level with steel wedges and packings, no larger than required, during the course of erection. The wedges and packings used should not obstruct the HD bolts or pockets. The space under the base plates is eventually packed with cement mortar after the erection of the steel framing or a sufficient part of it has been completed to the satisfaction of the Inspector.

It is important that the Inspector carefully checks all dimensions and levels during the setting out and construction of the foundations, as the accuracy of the lining and levelling of the erected steelwork depends on the foundations and HD bolts being in the correct positions. Particular attention should be paid to the height to which the HD bolts are set in the concrete bases, to avoid the situation where extension pieces have to be fitted to HD bolts due either to the concrete base level being too low, or to insufficient bolt projection allowed to permit washers and nuts being fitted to the bolts when the stanchions are erected and levelled. Conversely, too high a concrete base level will necessitate chipping the foundation back to the correct level. Rectifications of this nature are both costly and time-consuming and may delay the erection of the steelwork if the error is not detected and put right in time.

To provide some latitude in lateral dimensions and to facilitate lining up the stanchions when erected, HD bolts are not fixed rigidly in the concrete bases. The general practice is, whilst setting up bases for concreting, to form a pocket round the bolts by means of tapered timber boxes or strong waxed cardboard, plastic or similar tubes 75 mm or so in diameter, depending on the size of the bolts, extending from the steel anchorage material to just above the top of the concrete base. These tubes or boxes are removed after the base has been concreted and whilst the concrete is still green, the bolts being gently 'freed' at regular intervals whilst the concrete is setting. The holes in the concrete base are ultimately filled with cement grout during the final grouting of the steel base plate after erection, and small channels in the concrete, leading outwards from the bolt pockets, should be formed in the top of the concrete base to facilitate this operation.

It is important, on removal of the bolt boxes or tubes, that the bolt holes are firmly packed at the top with suitable removable packing material, to prevent the ingress of water and dirt.

It may be mentioned here that HD bolts are always provided with square heads, and with a short length of squared shank under the head for fitting into corresponding square holes in the anchorage material, to prevent rotation of the bolts when the nuts are tightened.

Steel base templates showing the position of the HD bolts are sometimes supplied by the steelwork contractor and may be useful for setting out small bases. For large bases the most satisfactory method of ensuring that the bolts are correctly positioned is for the general contractor to construct a skeleton timber frame at the top of the foundation, correctly lined and levelled, and with holes drilled in cross members at the requisite positions into which the HD bolts are threaded and thus retained in correct position during concreting.

All HD bolts and anchorage material to be embedded in concrete should be unpainted and free from grease or oil.

For steel members, such as beams bearing horizontally on walls, or similar supports where directional position is the main consideration, the general practice is to provide mortices during the construction of the concrete bearing pads into which rag bolts or similar fixings are inserted during the erection of the members concerned. The voids are filled with cement grout, as for stanchion bases, after lining up and levelling has been completed. Temporary spacers may sometimes be needed to keep a series of light beams in position, but in the majority of cases the weight of the beam itself is sufficient.

Unloading and stacking of materials

In view of the increased attention now being paid to the protection of steelwork against corrosion it is becoming universal practice for steelwork to be blast-cleaned and painted with at least a priming coat of paint before being despatched to site. Hence the importance of ensuring that as little damage as possible is done to the coated surfaces of the steelwork during transport to site, unloading and stacking, and subsequent handling for erection.

On arrival at site, except for items which can conveniently be dealt with by hand, the Inspector should see that materials are unloaded by crane, using nylon or suitably sheathed steel slings, and not rolled off and dumped from the transport vehicles.

The steelwork should be stacked on suitable softwood battens, clear of the ground and of any ponding which is likely to occur in wet weather. Battens should be placed between succeeding layers of steelwork, to avoid contact between painted surfaces, and regard should be paid to the order in which the stacked materials are required for erection.

Precaution against stacked materials being damaged by water or dirt should be taken by providing a suitable covering, sufficiently well ventilated to keep condensation to a minimum.

All specifications require that painted surfaces damaged during transport and unloading shall, without delay, be wire-brushed to a clean surface, and patch-primed with the original make of primer, the edges of the sound paintwork being feathered down with sandpaper to obtain a smooth surface after rectification.

The Inspector will decide on which areas need to be treated, having regard to the extent of the damage and the possibility of rust occurring before the final painting after erection. Areas of paintwork damaged during erection should be similarly dealt with before the final painting.

Steelwork to be embedded or encased in concrete is often blast-cleaned or wire-brushed before being sent to site, and similar precautions should be taken with regard to stacking and coverage to minimise the excessive formation of surface rust. Masking tape or other protection afforded in the works to the contact or faying surface of high strength friction grip (HSFG) bolt connections should be left in place and removed just prior to erection.

Erection

Prior to delivery of the steelwork to site the steelwork contractor should, in conjunction with the Inspector, check the setting out of the stanchion foundations and levels, and see that HD bolts are in their correct positions and loose in their pockets. A method often adopted as a means of assisting the placing of stanchions at their correct levels is the provision of small steel plate packings about 100 mm square, of the requisite thickness ascertained by levelling, these being set on the foundation blocks centrally under the stanchions at a level corresponding to the finished level of the underside of the stanchion base plates. The plates should be dead level in both directions and bedded in cement mortar as described on page 104 for grouting. This preliminary work will be the responsibility of the steelwork contractor and should be carried out sufficiently early to enable erection to proceed as planned.

The erection of structural steelwork is a skilled trade, carried out by experienced workmen, normally well versed in the methods and techniques of erecting structures of various kinds. The steelwork contractor is responsible for the suitability of all plant and equipment used for carrying out the erection, subject to the general approval of the Inspector. Cranes used for erection are usually of the mobile jib crane type, but the services of a tower crane may be required for the placing of steelwork at high levels.

The steelwork contractor is not to use equipment or methods of handling which, in the Inspector's opinion, may cause damage to the structure, including any substructure or superstructure. In the case of abnormal loads or sizes, the steelwork contractor should discuss with and obtain the Inspector's approval of the erection procedure to be adopted, bearing the above points in mind. Heavy members should not be rested on erected components or on light framing during the course of erection, and check ropes should be used to prevent members swinging during lifting. Nylon or suitable sheathed steel slings should be used for all lifting purposes to avoid damage to paintwork whilst the steelwork is being placed into position, and slings should be periodically checked for strength and defects during the course of the work.

Erection is generally begun by forming up to first floor level a stiff 'box' of stanchions with corresponding horizontal and lateral tie beams and floor beams, from which the erection is subsequently extended by stages in the desired direction. From the beginning, and at all stages of erection, special attention should be paid to the stability of the structure during erection and all precautions taken against collapse. If necessary, and where permanent bracing is not provided, temporary bracing should be fitted so as to make adequate provision for all erection stresses and conditions, including wind, and those due to erection equipment and its operation. Reliance should not be placed on HD bolts for temporarily holding stanchions in vertical positions prior to the erection and connection of stabilising members. Such stanchions, and other unsupported members, should be adequately stayed during the initial operations, as the accidental overturning of an unsupported stanchion could have a disastrous effect on the HD bolts and bases. Permanent bolts may be used temporarily for initial erection purposes, provided a sufficient number of bolts is fitted in each connection and properly tightened, but HSFG bolts used as erection bolts should not be tightened more than is sufficient to bring the surfaces into close contact and, if necessary, service bolts should be used and replaced by HSFG bolts later. It will be one of the duties of the Inspector to check, during the final stages of erection and whilst lining, levelling and plumbing is being completed, that all remaining bolts are inserted and that all connections are a close fit, with bolts permanently tightened, having regard to the special tightening operation required for HSFG bolts. For steel framed buildings with cladded sides and roof, permanent bracing between stanchions and roof members is invariably provided in the end bays and, depending on the length of the building, in selected intermediate bays. During erection of the roof trusses, or frames, care should be taken to see that trusses are held firmly in position until the roof purlins are fitted and bolted, either by the use of the bracing provided, or by using selected lengths of purlins as temporary bracings in other bays.

For structures where side walls are to be filled in with brickwork or other construction, temporary mild steel angle cross bracings should be provided for each line of main stanchions, and left in position until at least two or more bays, as the Inspector may decide, are completed up to roof or eaves level, the temporary bracing being subsequently removed by the steelwork contractor.

No rectification of steelwork, cleats or fittings, found to be necessary without approval by the Inspector, who will decide in each case whether rectification can be carried out satisfactorily by welding up and re-drilling at site, or whether defective members should be altered at works, or replaced. The use of an excessive number of washers to accommodate errors in fabrication should not be permitted.

Where large framed units, such as latticed girders and trusses, are sent in pieces for assembling and bolting together on site before erection, care should be taken to see that any camber specified is achieved on finally assembling. Interconnecting members should be eased into place and light drifting only with minimum force should be permitted to bring holes into alignment. Surfaces which will be in contact when assembled should be given a coat of the original primer paint before assembling, except interfaces where connections are made by means of HSFG bolts.

Holes badly in misalignment should not be heavily drifted, or reamed. The cause of misalignment should be checked by the Inspector and if not due to incorrect assembly, the members involved should be rectified or replaced.

All holes required for site modifications, additional site connections or missed during fabrication should be drilled unless it is decided that welding will be adopted. No thermal cutting equipment should be used on site without the Inspector's express permission.

In special cases where, for erection purposes, larger than normal end clearances have been allowed at the ends of beams, properly shaped steel packings should be used and fitted, to obtain a tight connection to the Inspector's satisfaction.

Lining and levelling

The steelwork contractor is responsible for placing each part of the structure in its correct position, properly lined, levelled and plumbed, and no riveting, welding or permanent bolting should be carried out until correct alignment of the steelwork has been achieved to the satisfaction of the Inspector.

Stanchion bases are levelled and plumbed by means of wedging and packing as has been previously described, and similar methods apply to steel beams bearing on wall pads. Large and heavy stanchion bases are sometimes provided, during fabrication, with stout levelling screws at the corners of the base, for screwing down onto steel packs on the concrete. The use of these screws greatly facilitates the operation of levelling and plumbing. If the stanchions are correctly levelled and centred, beams will automatically come into line if the steelwork has been accurately fabricated. Spot checks should be given to height of beam from time to time, particularly in cases where minimum clearance heights of openings are specified. Larger bases will also be provided with holes about 50 mm diameter in appropriate positions in the central area of the base plate, to allow escape of air and facilitate grouting.

Lining up will be carried out by checking lateral and longitudinal centres of stanchion, and taking appropriate diagonal dimensions to ensure that the structure is 'square', the stanchions being levered into correct alignment as may be necessary. Apart from making dimensional checks, the Inspector should be constantly making visual checks by sighting with the eye along rows of stanchions, or top surface of beams, when any misalignment will be immediately apparent and can be investigated. A spirit level is a useful instrument for the Inspector to carry around for rough spot checks on plumbs and levels. An approved steel tape should be used at all times for taking or checking dimensions.

Where extreme accuracy is necessary, as for instance in the alignment of crane gantry tracks, a theodolite will probably be required for use in obtaining a true line, but the crane gantry girders themselves should be found level if the supporting stanchions have been accurately levelled. It would be advisable for the Inspector to check this work in conjunction with the steelwork contractor whilst any necessary adjustments are made to crane girder diaphragm connections involving the slackening and re-tightening of bolts, the possible introduction of packings, etc, and to re-check the readings after each stage has been completed. At the same time, the correct span between crane rails should be maintained and this should be checked from time to time, using a steel tape or a length of piano wire marked with the correct span. Crane rails are generally fastened to the crane girders by means of special bolted clips, and the adjustment of rails should not present any problem. Ends of crane rails are usually cut at an angle of forty-five degrees and joints should abut tightly. No grouting of stanchion bases or beams bearing on walls should be carried out until the lining, levelling and plumbing of the steelwork has been completed to the Inspector's satisfaction.

For normal structural steelwork the permissible tolerances within which the final position of the steelwork can be accepted are typically as follows:

Linear dimensions (in plan)
up to and including 8 metres	± 10 mm
over 8 m up to and including 15 m	± 15 mm
over 15 m	± 20 mm
over 25 m	± 25 mm

Plumb

Maximum permissible deviation (PD)
in 30 m height   ± 15 mm

Levels

Permissible deviation between designed
and actual level of the base of the first
stanchion to be erected   ± 5 mm

PD between designed and actual level
of any beam at its junction with a
stanchion, in any 30 m length   ± 15 mm

PD between designed and actual levels
of two or more beams meeting at a
stanchion   ± 5 mm

The tolerances specified are not cumulative. Erection tolerances are frequently laid down in the specification for the steelwork concerned, and the Inspector should then be guided by the figures stipulated in the specification.

Grouting

Immediately before grouting, spaces under the steel bases or girder bearings should be thoroughly cleaned. Bedding of stanchion bases and the bearing of beams and girders on stone, brick and plain or reinforced concrete walls should be carried out by the general contractor.

Using cement grout to a thickness of between 25 mm to 50 mm as required: the grout should not be leaner than 1:2 cement and sand and should be mixed as thickly as possible consistent with fluidity. It should be poured under a suitable head and tamped until the space to be grouted, including holding down bolt pockets is completely filled. Suitable barriers should be formed round the edges of the area to be grouted to prevent the grout running out from under the base.

Other permissible alternatives for grouting are thickly mixed neat cement mortar to a thickness not exceeding 25 mm, or using cement mortar not leaner than cement to fine aggregate 1:2, mixed as dry as possible and having a thickness of not less than 50 mm, consolidated by thoroughly ramming with a blunt rammer against firm supports until the space is completely filled. This latter method will not be suitable for filling in holding down bolt pockets.

For multi-storey buildings, grouting may be permitted when a sufficient number of bottom lengths of stanchions have been properly lined, levelled and plumbed, and a sufficient number of floor beams are in position as decided by the Inspector. Similar considerations may be applied to the erection by stages of steelwork for other buildings.

Accommodation of services

Holes for service pipes and conduits, usually in the webs of beams, are generally drilled at the steel contractor's works from information supplied in advance by the specialist sub-contractors concerned. However, it frequently occurs that due to late information, or modification of layout, etc, additional holes require to be provided at site in the erected steelwork. Such holes should preferably be drilled, but, whilst this is not to be encouraged, random small diameter holes, say up to 40 mm diameter may be formed by careful gas cutting, at the discretion of the Inspector, always provided that such holes are formed on the centre lines of beam webs and that the strength of the beam is not affected. Where larger diameter holes are required, the matter should be referred to Head Office for a decision as to whether the holes are permissible, where and how they shall be cut, and whether any compensating rings or plates are to be fitted to the member concerned. No notching should be permitted in beam flanges.

Encased steelwork

Steelwork to be embedded or encased in concrete is invariably erected unpainted, but all loose mill-scale and rust should be removed by thorough wire-brushing, and all surfaces cleaned free of contamination from oil, grease or paint, immediately before the steelwork is placed in position for concreting. Steelwork cleaned in the fabricator's works, prior to delivery to site, should have any surface rust or contamination incurred during storage removed in a similar manner.

Protection of floor slabs

When erecting on or over concrete or other floors, the steelwork contractor should take steps to prevent damage occurring to the floors through careless handling of steel members, or bolts, spanners and lifting tackle. If it is necessary to run erection cranes over ground floors permission should be obtained from the Inspector, and protection should be provided to prevent damage to the floors. Where circumstances and the construction programme permits, laying of floors in areas where erection cranes require to operate should not be carried out until lifting operations are completed.

Safety regulations

The Inspector should see that all safety regulations in force are observed during the course of erection. When the erection of the steelwork has been completed to the Inspector's satisfaction, the structure can be released for painting, subject to prior requirements of other trades before painting is put in hand.

High strength friction grip (HSFG) bolts

High strength friction grip bolts have largely superseded rivets and other methods of fastening used for making joints or major connections between structural members at site. A joint formed with HSFG bolts derives its strength from frictional effect between the interfacing or 'faying' surfaces, rather than by shearing or bearing action on the bolts. The principle of HSFG bolts is that when properly tightened, the bolts develop a sufficiently high clamping force on the joint to carry the working loads by the friction developed between the contact surfaces, the bolts being subject to tensile stresses only and the loads governed by the axial bolt tension.

A type of bolt commonly used in structural steelwork is the load indicating bolt (LIB), which has the advantage that it needs only a simple inspection to determine whether the bolt has been properly tightened.

Load indicating bolts have square heads, with small raised pads under the head at each corner. Before tightening, the head contacts the steelwork with its four corners only, leaving gaps under the head on its four sides. When the bolts are tightened by spanner or impact tool, the gap is gradually closed by yielding of the metal in the head, until the manufacturer's recommended gap for minimum bolt tension has been achieved. Hardened steel washers should be placed under the nut, or under the head of the bolt, whichever of these two components is to be rotated during the tightening operation.

In bolts of a typical manufacturer the specified minimum load is induced in the bolt when the gap width is closed to 1.0 mm. As there is no detriment in the bolts being further tightened, when it is required to seal the bolt heads by painting, closing the gap to 0.5 mm is recommended, and in the type of steelwork we are considering this is the condition which will generally apply. In all cases, the bolt manufacturer's recommended width of gaps should be strictly adhered to.

Where HSFG bolts pass through members with tapered flanges suitable hardened tapered washers should be used to render the bearing surfaces parallel, and the bolts inserted so that the washer is under the non-rotating component.

Load-indicating washers are employed in some instances instead of load-indicating bolts, but the principles outlined above remain essentially the same.

Contact surfaces of HSFG bolt connections should not be painted or bear traces of oil or grease, and no gasket or other flexible material should be placed between the joint. The Inspector should see that, immediately prior to assembly the surfaces are free from rust and loose particles, and if necessary wire-brushed to present smooth and clean mating surfaces before the joint is made.

HSFG bolts may be used temporarily in erection to facilitate assembly by tightening the bolts sufficiently to bring members into close contact, but the bolts should not be finally tightened until after the structure has been lined and levelled.

On final tightening, the bolts or nuts should be tightened in a staggered pattern, and in large joints they should be tightened from the centre of the joint outwards. The only inspection required is to see that the gaps under the bolt heads have been closed to the specified dimension. This can be done visually with the assistance of a 'no-go' feeler gauge of requisite thickness to check borderline cases. Once fully tightened to the correct gap and for any reason subsequently slackened off, HSFG bolts, nuts and washers should be discarded and not re-used.

Where load indicating components are not used the bolts have to be tightened to a specified torque by pre-set hand impact tools, the torque being that which imparts the required shank tension to the bolt. It is usual practice to keep a master torque wrench in the steelwork contractor's office and to calibrate daily the hand impact tools against the master torque wrench, each type being adjusted to 'break' at the required torque. It may be considered necessary to check the calibration of the hand tools more than once daily. A manufacturer's test certificate guaranteeing the accuracy of the master torque wrench is essential. The serial numbers of all tools used should be recorded.

Once a tightened bolt has been tested and approved, it is usually marked by coloured paint to signify its acceptance. As with all HSFG bolts it is essential that every bolt in every joint be tested and approved, not just a sample from each joint.

Bolting

The use of HSFG bolts for making major connections at site has already been described.

Black bolts and nuts are commonly used, with the appropriate washers, for members carrying lighter loads, and for fixing in position members where the resistance to shear on the connection is already provided by cleats or brackets welded on during fabrication.

The main points for the Inspector to note are as follows: All bolts should be fitted with a washer under the nut, and where necessary, suitable tapered washers fitted under the washer or under the head of the bolt, to give a true bearing on tapered flanges of joints and channels or similar members.

The bolt projection through the nut should be not less than two full threads after the washers have been fitted and the bolts tightened, the nearest standard length of bolt to be used complying with the requirement.

In cases where the full bearing area of the bolt is to be developed,

107

the unthreaded shank of the bolt should project through the bolt hole, suitably thick washers being provided to enable the bolt to be tightened.

Suitable spring washers should be fitted under nuts for connecting suspended members or hangers, or in cases where nuts are liable to work loose in members subject to vibration. During the assembling of members for bolting, only 'podgering' or light drifting should be permitted to bring bolt holes into correct alignment. Heavy drifting resulting in the enlargement of holes and distortion of members should be stopped and the cause investigated.

Some specifications may require bolts and nuts to be dipped in linseed oil before use, and this should be checked by the Inspector. In any event, the specification will require that bolts, nuts, washers and other fastenings eventually receive the same protective treatment as provided for the steelwork.

The permanent bolting should not be done until proper alignment of the steelwork has been obtained.

The Inspector should positively check that the correct type and grade of bolt is being used at each connection and should keep samples of each type of bolt, nut and washer in his office for identification purposes.

Precision bolts, which are superior to black bolts, are another grade of bolt commonly used in structural steelwork.

Riveting

Riveting as a means of connecting members in ordinary structural steelwork has largely been superseded by the shop welding of components and the jointing of these together at site by means of HSFG bolts, nuts and washers previously described. In circumstances, however, in which site-riveting forms part of the specifications, or is otherwise required, the Inspector should see that the following procedure is observed:

Members to be riveted should be securely bolted together with service bolts sufficient in number to keep the member firmly in place before and during riveting, and with all holes in correct alignment.

Special care should be given to single riveted connections by clamping the members securely together and supporting them as necessary during riveting.

Rivets should be uniformly heated throughout their length without burning or excessive scaling, and should be of sufficient length to enable heads of standard dimensions to be formed, concentric with the shaft.

The length of the rivets should be such as to avoid small or ill-formed heads, or heads with rings of surplus metal at the base.

Special care should be taken in the heating and driving of long rivets.

Wherever practicable site rivets should be driven by pneumatic tools, powered by a suitable portable air compressor. Only in cases where circumstances or site conditions render it unavoidable should riveting by hand tools be permitted, necessitating particular care and attention being paid to the above points.

All loose, burned, or defectively formed rivets should be cut out and replaced during riveting operations. Care should be taken in cutting off heads and removing shanks of defective rivets to avoid distortion or damage to members and the enlargement of rivet holes, the latter probably resulting in a larger replacement rivet being required.

Apart from the obvious defects referred to, rivets should be inspected for tightness by tapping the heads sharply with a light hammer, the resulting high metallic 'ring' being immediately discernable from the dull 'ring' of a loose rivet. Special care should be taken to inspect all single-riveted connections.

Caulking of loose rivets or rivets with badly formed heads should not be permitted. Such rivets should be cut out and replaced.

It should be noted that site riveting may possibly create a fire hazard under certain site conditions, and the Inspector should see that suitable precautions are taken in appropriate cases.

Site welding

Whilst it too has largely superseded riveting in the building up of specialised forms of steel construction, welding does not figure very largely as a site operation in the type of structure under consideration in this chapter. It is, however, almost universally used for workshop fabrications, with the major joints at site being made by means of HSFG bolts as previously described. Site welding can, however, provide a useful means of effecting alterations, or in making provision for extra members and supports required due to changed requirements or additions to the work, eliminating the necessity for drilling holes for connections.

Site welding generally involves the use of a portable electric welding transformer, for which power should be available or provided on the site.

The method of welding will be subject to the approval of the Inspector. The steelwork contractor is responsible for all welding work, which should be carried out by competent welders and evidence of their competency produced if required before any welding is carried out. Such evidence may take the form of welders certificates or the preparation of standard test pieces chosen to simulate the type of welding required in practice, eg overhead work, vertical-up, vertical-horizontal, on pipe and plate.

The issuing of welders certificates of competence and the approval of test pieces is done by accredited bodies authorised in this field.

Welds should be made by the metal arc process, using electrodes suitable for the work. All electrodes should be stored in a dry place.

The steelwork contractor should provide expert supervision for the whole of the work and afford every facility for the Inspector to check the work during execution.

The size and type of weld, together with the surface preparation required for each member or part to be welded, will be subject to the Inspector's approval, and copies of drawings and any relevant instructions regarding the welding should be supplied to the Inspector for inspection purposes. All members or connections should be free from any twist or distortion when the welding is completed, and suitable approved welding procedures adopted to achieve this end. No welding should be permitted in unsuitable weather conditions, or when the air temperature falls to less than 2°C.

After cooling, if the welding has been completed to the Inspector's satisfaction, the weld should be chipped clean of slag using a light hammer, the weld and surrounding areas thoroughly wire-brushed, and painted with a coat of suitable primer prior to subsequent overcoating with the specified paint system.

All welding operations carried out in the vicinity of other work, or workmen, should be suitably screened, and all necessary precautions taken against the risk of fire.

Blast cleaning at site

The necessity for blast cleaning steelwork at site does not arise in the case of the type of structure under consideration in this chapter, where blast cleaning will already have been carried out at works before or after fabrication, but a few general notes may be found helpful in case the question arises where existing steelwork is involved. Blast cleaning should be carried out, unless otherwise specified, to BS 4232 second quality. The maximum surface profile and amplitude for surfaces to be painted should be 100 microns (amplitude is the depth of blast-cleaning profile from trough to peak). In some circumstances a lower profile may be specified. Expendable silica-free abrasive will be specified for the blasting operations, of a size such that the maximum surface profile amplitude of 100 microns is not exceeded.

An instantaneous recovery machine should be employed, otherwise the cleaned steel surface should be air blasted with clean dry air, vacuum cleaned with an industrial type machine, or otherwise freed from residues and dust immediately after blast cleaning. Blast cleaning should not be carried out in areas close to painting operations and wet coated surfaces, unless effectively screened, to prevent the spread of abrasive particles contaminating the paint film. For on-site blasting under open conditions, in addition to the above consideration, the work should be carried out so that no damage is caused to any machinery or moving parts in the vicinity of the blasting operations.

Any oil or grease on the steel surfaces should be removed by white spirit or other approved solvent prior to the commencement of blast cleaning. The steel surfaces should be perfectly dry, and the atmospheric conditions such that condensation does not occur on the steel before the blast cleaning has been completed and the surfaces cleaned and primed. The work entails the use of a suitable portable air compressor, and the compressed air should be dry and free from oil.

Immediately after blasting, or within not more than two hours under suitable weather conditions, all blast cleaned steel surfaces should be painted with a coat of protective priming paint, and then subsequently coated according to the requirements of the painting specification.

If from any cause rust is allowed to form on the surfaces before priming, the surfaces should be re-blasted before priming.

Site painting of structural steelwork

The Inspector deputed to supervise the site painting of the erected steelwork should have had wide practical experience of the types of paints used and the application procedures involved. Often, an independent firm specialising in this field is engaged to undertake the work.

The painting of structural steelwork covers a very wide field, and the subject including the duties of the Inspector and the keeping of records, is dealt with exhaustively in BS 5493: — 'Code of Practice for Protective Coating of Iron and Steel Structures against Corrosion' (formerly CP 2008), to which reference should be made.

The Inspector should make a careful study of this specification, and a copy should be kept available for use on site.

Many variable factors are involved in the site painting of structural steelwork, eg the type of structure, types of paints and number of coats required, film thicknesses and drying times, environmental and climatic conditions, etc, and it is impracticable to lay down standard requirements in the form of a general specification as is the case with the steelwork itself and other construction materials.

No two projects are exactly the same in the above respect, and the various requirements should be laid down clearly in the form of a contract specification applying to the particular work concerned.

Before going on to give an example of requirements which a typical painting specification may contain, it may be useful to explain the unit 'micron', almost universally used for indicating the thickness of paint films immediately after application (wet film thickness) or after the paint has dried out (dry film thickness and usually abbreviated to DFT). Both are interrelated, the dry film thickness naturally depending on the thickness to which the wet paint is laid, but the ultimate 'dry film thickness' is the one with which specifications are mainly concerned.

Paint film thicknesses are sometimes alternatively expressed in thousandths of an inch (or 'mils') *viz* 0.001″, etc, and, more latterly, in fractions of a millimeter.

The symbol used for the micron is the Greek letter μ, and the relationship between the various units is as follows: 1 micron = 1m x 10^{-6} = 1 μm.

100 microns = 0.004″(4 mils) = 0.10 millimetres approx.

Hence 0.001″ (1 mil) = 25 microns = 0.025 mm approx.

Details of recommended wet and dry film thicknesses, and the approximate surface area which can be covered by unit quantities of paint applied at these thicknesses, after allowing for application losses, are given in the manufacturer's technical data sheets for the paints concerned.

The measurement of paint film thicknesses is an essential part of the Inspector's duties, and the methods and gauges used for the purpose are fully described in BS 5493.

Painting specifications

Specifications drawn up for a particular work, besides giving the makes and type of paints to be used, the number of coats required, and the dry film thickness to be achieved with each coat, will include requirements relating to the execution of the work, of which the following are typical:

Surfaces

Any damage caused to primed steelwork surfaces during erection should be cleaned and patch primed, and the paint restored to its original condition before further painting is carried out.

Surfaces should be clean and dry before painting. Any accumulation of dirt or mud acquired on surfaces during erection should be removed by a mild soapy solution, washed off with cold water and allowed to dry. Accumulation of grease or oil should be removed with white spirit.

Storage of paint

Paints should be stored in sealed containers in a paint store not exposed to extreme temperatures. Paints should be thoroughly mixed before use and no dilution by thinners will be permitted except in accordance with the maker's recommendations and the

Inspector's approval. Paint should be supplied from the store ready for application.

Application of paint

Painting should be carried out by skilled painters, under competent supervision.

Manufacturer's data sheets shall be strictly followed in respect to film thicknesses, drying and overcoating times, etc. Each coat of paint should be allowed to harden properly before the next coat is applied.

To ensure that the dry film thickness required will be met, the wet film paint thickness of areas being coated should, during application, be regularly checked by the Inspector to enable immediate adjustment to be made if the film thickness is too low and to avoid the necessity of paint being subsequently worked up. The dry film thickness of coated areas should also be regularly checked and, where deficient, brought up to the specified thickness by further paint application before overcoating is permitted.

Paint should not be applied under the following conditions:

(a) When the ambient temperature falls below 5°C.

(b) When the relative humidity rises above ninety per cent.

(c) When the surfaces are wet with rain or snow, or during fog or mist.

(d) When condensation has occurred, or is likely to occur, due to the temperature of the steel surfaces falling below the dew point of the atmosphere.

No painting is to be carried out on damp or wet surfaces or, where due to weather conditions, on surfaces which are likely to become wet before the painting is completed.

Before application of a succeeding coat of paint, the previously painted surface should be dust-free. Cleaned surfaces should be painted the same day, otherwise the Inspector may require them to be re-cleaned before painting.

All bolts, nuts and washers in the erected steelwork should receive the same protective treatment as applied to the steelwork, and particular care should be given to maintaining strong paint film on such fastenings and on all cleats and arrises and to areas around attachments and joints.

In structures where surfaces of steelwork will subsequently be concealed by cladding or lining, the full protective treatment should be applied to the surfaces before any cladding or similar work is carried out. The Inspector should take note of any special provisions made in the specification for additional treatment to such surfaces.

Finishing coats of paint should not be applied until the installation is complete and the area free from dust.

Paints may only be applied by spray in suitable cases, otherwise paints should be applied by brush. Spraying will not be permitted where overspray is likely to cause damage to surfaces of any adjoining construction.

Throughout the work the Inspector should check that:

1   surfaces have been properly prepared;
2   the paint is being applied in accordance with the manufacturer's instructions;
3   the weather conditions are suitable for painting;
4   the required film thicknesses are being obtained;
5   any records required are regularly maintained.

7 Earthworks

Brickwork, concrete, steelwork, bituminous paving and earthworks together account for the majority of construction works. Of these, brickwork, concrete and bituminous pavings have been variously covered in other sections of this book rather than having separate chapters devoted to them each because knowledge of construction in these materials is widespread. Structural steelwork is also a widely used material but warrants a chapter of its own because of its distinctive method of use, that is, it arrives on site prefabricated and ready for erection in contrast to the other aforementioned materials which are, usually, formed on the site itself prior to their being employed in construction. Strictly speaking, bricks may not be so described but being individually small and requiring a site-made material (mortar), they are included in the category of site-made materials. Earthworks being so distinctly a different and separate site activity also warrant a chapter to themselves.

The workings of the earthworks section is often regarded as something of a mystery by the rest of the contract. One day their plant is here, there and everywhere, apparently roaming about in all directions, the next day they are nowhere to be seen. The object of this chapter is to describe step by step, the routine of earthworks as they would be organised on large works, for instance in the construction of an earth fill dam or a large river training embankment. The methods described also apply equally to other projects, airfield or motorway construction for example, where earthmoving may form a substantial part of the contract. Canals are rather a special case and usually entail large scale cut and fill operations.

Supervision and inspection of earthworks needs to be systematic and should match the Contractor's methods of working as described in the foregoing paragraphs. Supervision and inspection will normally proceed in two parallel concurrent divisions which for convenience may be described as (a) field control and (b) laboratory control. As with other forms of construction, control may be as formal or as informal as desired to suit particular circumstances and preferences. Formal procedures lead generally to better records and are not, as is so often thought, a restraint or hinderance to smooth progress of the works. On large contracts formal procedures are almost essential if programmes are to be kept. Informal procedures are better suited to smaller works or small sections of large projects. Whatever the size of project it is always an advantage to be in at the beginning of operations when construction and control procedures

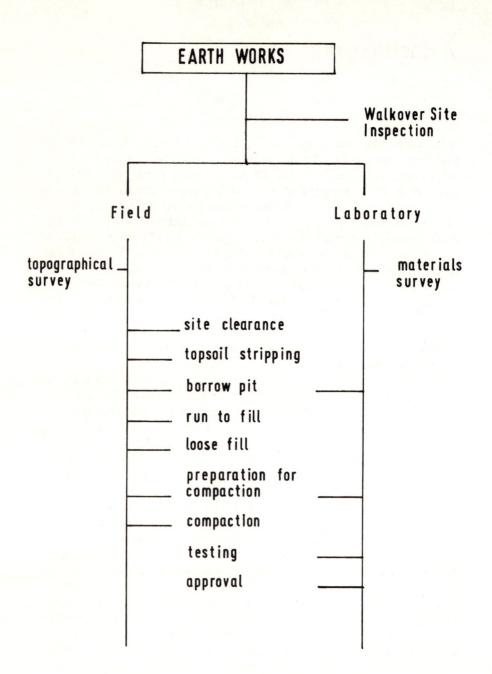

Diagram 7

116

are still being established. It is also valuable from the point of view of present construction and future reference to know the lie of the land before it is altered by the works.

Field control should be exercised and records maintained appertaining to the various criteria which relate to the various stages and aspects of construction described, eg levels, depth of loose fill, moisture content, suitability and uniformity of fill, compaction.

Laboratory control should be similarly exercised, being especially concerned with soil characteristics, moisture content, relative compaction, densities and soil gradings. As these two divisions of control proceed interdependently and simultaneously it will be appreciated that on a sizeable project all this supervision and testing gives rise to a considerable amount of data. This data needs to be recorded in a systematic way, not only for future reference but more especially for immediate use in the day to day control of the works. Progress drawings, graphs and charts are the tools of this control and are described in chapter 2, Records.

This present chapter is divided into the following broad sections:

1 Site inspection
2 Site clearance
3 Site investigations
4 General site preparation
5 General procedure
6 Plant
7 Miscellaneous

1 Site inspection

Even before the earthmoving plant arrives on site the opportunity should be taken for inspecting the site or route that the works are to take. In this inspection likely trouble spots should be noted in a book or on a map for further investigation and survey prior to the commencement of works. Such trouble spots could be, for example, ponds, ditches, or creeks lying across the route. As with conventional sites, an original ground level survey will be necessary, executed jointly by Contractor and Inspector and these surveys, besides recording general topography and ground levels, will also record ditches, river bed levels and the like. Once ground levels have been recorded the way is clear for site clearance and top soil stripping to commence, but before these activities are described a word or two is required regarding the arrival of the earthmoving plant itself.

The plant, in all its varieties, may arrive under its own power or on transporters. The date of arrival of the various machines, their type and condition should be noted as should also the dates they start work. A walk around the Contractor's plant yard to inspect the condition and state of preparation of the plant is well worth while. This should be done not only on the plant's first arrival but also at periodic intervals throughout construction for record purposes and to form an opinion of the reliability which may be expected in current and future operations. Do not be deceived by a fresh coat of paint on an old machine.

2 Site clearance

Prior to commencement of site clearance and top soil stripping agreed sites for top soil tips and spoil heaps should be established and recorded. These sites should be inspected and surveyed prior to use not only for future record and measurement purposes but also to verify that their establishment will not endanger existing or future works nor create hazards to existing property. Top soil tips will normally be removed in the course of events when topsoiling operations begin but spoil heaps may be either temporary or permanent depending on circumstances and on the conditions of agreements reached with landowners prior to their establishment. Top soil tips and spoil heaps, temporary or permanent, should be marked on the plans as they are established.

Site clearance is arguably the most untidy of times, when the site may resemble a battlefield. It is the time when buildings are demolished, trees felled, hedges grubbed out, roads and streams diverted, known or unknown existing services uncovered for diversion, etc. All these features should of course appear on the contract drawings but there may be omissions so it is important that all such features are recorded; houses measured (ground plan and storey height and general description usually suffices plus a photograph); major trees noted for number and girth; roads and tracks for width and construction; cross sections of ditches, etc. An important point to guard against is the casual filling, during site clearance, of small ditches, gullies and such like which can so easily happen inadvertently in the general untidiness of site clearance operations. This is why the recording of such items is so important during the site survey before site clearance commences.

Grubbing out hedges usually presents no problems but the grubbing out of tree roots can be a major task, leaving areas of disturbed ground which require extensive compaction operations often to a depth of two or three metres.

Top soil stripping takes over where site clearance finishes. Depending on the terrain in question, stripping may be necessary to a depth of say 150 mm, or a depth of 500 mm or more may be required in some locations. To establish the depth of top soil removal required reference should be made, in the first instance, to the drawings, specification or bill of quantities and any quoted figure then verified by trial holes on site. It is important that the top soil is adequately removed and that a record is kept of the actual depths worked to. Judging the depth of cut by eye is one way of doing this, but an unreliable way. The depth of cut judged against original ground level at the edge of cut may not be the same as that in mid field. The only sure way of ascertaining the depth of stripping is to take and agree levels after top soil removal is complete, it is convenient if the before and after levels are taken on the same grid to assist comparisons.

3 Site investigations

Concurrent with the establishment of the foregoing procedures will be the site investigations, sampling, testing and approval of borrow pit locations for embankment construction. The location of suitable material will have been determined in the precontract site investigation and design stage but now will be the time when suitable borrow pits are located and opened up. The location, depth and dimensions of the pits themselves may be restricted in the specification and these items should be checked when the Contractor's proposals are received.

The sites of the borrow pits will require stripping of top soil and the removal of any unsuitable material before the approved material may be won. The material is usually sampled from test pits, scraper cuts or other large open excavation to enable a good visual inspection, as well as laboratory analyses, to be carried out. Assuming a borrow pit is approved and used, regular inspection and sampling is required as the pit is extended to ensure that material won from it remains within the specification. If unsuitable material is encountered in an approved pit the unsuitable material will require removal before the pit is approved for use again. Factors which can determine the extent of borrow pit development are excavating plant economics and the ground water table. Borrow pits should be surveyed before and after use for recording on drawings and for a quantities check though, by their nature, no great accuracy is possible or necessary. Borrow pits should not be located in areas where they may adversely affect future extensions of the permanent works.

The motor scraper, of which more later, is the most common machine used in earthwork operations but for winning materials below the water table, such as sands for use in filter zones, a dragline is used. A dragline in the hands of a skilled operator can achieve high outputs to stockpile which should not be overlooked in routine materials sampling. Otherwise significant quantities of out of specification material may go into the works undetected, or only be detected in situ rather than in the stockpile.

4 General site preparation

The activities of site survey, site clearance and top soil stripping, already mentioned in previous chapters, are followed by the preparation of the formation before general filling commences.

Prior to this, ponds, watercourses and such like will require

119

careful treatment by way of de-watering, cleaning out and controlled filling to general ground level before fill may be laid over them.
In cleaning out it is important to check that all soft material is properly removed to a satisfactory depth before filling is permitted and
a close watch kept on the behaviour of the fill as it is laid. Soft
underlying areas will soon show up by the rutting and heaving of the
fill. Levels should be taken prior to filling so that the volume of fill
placed in the watercourse can be determined. In some circumstances,
and with certain materials, it may be permissible not to de-water the
watercourse but to muck it out by dragline and deposit fill in the
standing water. If this is permitted a trial pit(s) should be opened
as soon as practical in the deposited material to check density and
compaction. The pit should extend to below bed level so that the
efficiency of mucking out may be inspected. Those areas noted in
early surveys as being possibly troublesome should now also be
checked and cut out as necessary together with any others which
may have become apparent during site clearance and stripping. It
is important that all such areas should be located on the plans and
surveyed for record and measurement purposes. Having dealt with
all watercourses, areas of soft ground and the like, the way will now
be clear for subgrade compaction and formation treatment before
the placing of the first layers of fill proper commences. Firstly,
filling will commence in local low areas, bringing them up to the
general prevailing level before being extended to cover the full section
in question, width and length. Cut from borrow pits or from sections
of works lying in cut, assuming the material to be suitable, will then
be run to fill and spread, levelled, adjusted for moisture content
and compacted, all in a repetitious sequence until the correct
embankment profile has been achieved. That in outline is the basic
procedure of earthmoving and now each separate part of that procedure, namely running cut to fill, spreading, levelling, adjustment
for moisture content and, lastly, compaction will be considered
separately with regard to the different elements of supervision
required in each and some remarks concerning the plant commonly
used.

5   General procedure

Filling; Preparation for compaction; Compaction; Testing
The description that follows assumes the filling of an earth embankment by motor scraper, probably the most common and familiar
of earthmoving operations. Embankments may be built of materials
other than earth fill, soft rocks such as chalk and shale being in
common use where available. Such other materials are commonly
run to fill in dump trucks loaded by face shovel or front end loader
and are spread and levelled by bulldozer. Their compaction then
follows the same procedures used for earth fill. It is not the intent

of this chapter to describe the theory and practice of earthmoving operations except in so far that a knowledge of the routine is required in order to explain the pattern of supervision and where and why it is required. This routine, consisting of the sequential operations of filling, preparation for compaction, compaction itself and lastly testing is now described taking each operation in turn. The preceeding operations of site clearance and top soil stripping common to most construction projects whatever their type, have already been described.

Filling

Running cut to fill is probably the most familiar sight of an earthmoving operation. It starts with the impressive, noisy sight of the scraper loading, with perhaps the assistance of a tractor or even two, then the loaded scraper running fast to the filling area and discharging its load with scarcely a break in pace, and lastly its even faster return run to the loading area. In earthmoving, as in all construction activities, speed is money and the scraper routes will have been arranged to provide as fast a cycle of operations as possible; no wonder then that the imposition of quality control on these operations might appear a daunting task.

The suitability of the material being loaded is checked by regular inspection of the borrow areas as they are developed, inspection being by both visual and laboratory examination. It is useful if samples of material, approved by testing in the laboratory, are held available on site so that visual comparison is readily made when changes of material are encountered. The samples should cover the range from excellent to totally unsuitable and limits of acceptance and rejection indicated. A strict record should be kept of where the material from each particular borrow area is deposited in the works, recording chainage, level and width. Comparative laboratory testing of the material should be made to establish correlation between results obtained in the borrow area and as laid. If restrictions have been specified regarding the dimensions, depth or clearances of the borrow area these should be checked as cutting proceeds.

The haul route from borrow area to fill area will be the optimum that the Contractor can devise under any given circumstances and it is very much in his own interests to maintain it so. Due regard should be given to the interests of safety, not only of the works themselves but also to the general public, and this latter point is especially relevant where haul routes cross public roads. Temporary traffic lights, signs and other controls should be discussed with police and local authority and the agreed standards should be maintained, and checked to see that they are being maintained. Traffic control will also be necessary on the site roads themselves, priority usually being given to the haul traffic for obvious reasons in view of the size of

121

the vehicles employed.

As an embankment rises, temporary access ramps may be required, the location of these will be chosen to suit the length of sections being worked. There is generally no restriction on the location of these ramps, other than those obviously dictated by the works, but removal of the ramps does require more attention and planning. By the time the ramps come to be removed, access to them may be restricted and some disturbance to the face of the embankment adjacent to the ramps is almost inevitable, requiring remedial work which in itself may be awkward to execute. Another point is that the increase in embankment height is usually associated with a reduction in embankment width. This reduction in width may cause access problems for the earthmoving plant which though usually quite manoeuverable are nevertheless bulky vehicles and their turning and scuffing will disturb previously compacted and approved work which will consequently require making good.

When the scraper arrives at the area being filled it will be directed to the correct lane and start of lay point and then discharge its load evenly as it travels. The specification will limit the depth to which loose fill may be laid, 300 mm being a common value for general fill, and this is the first point to check. Normally, although perhaps the most obvious control to be exercised, controlling the depth of loose fill is seldom a problem because too thick a layer merely hinders the passage of the discharging scraper, and its followers, along its path. By the time a section has been filled and graded level the specification depth is seldom exceeded significantly. It is prudent nevertheless to check the average thickness of layers every so often, rather than individually, and note whilst so doing whether the specification limits the individual layer in loose depth or compacted depth.

The quality of the material being laid should be inspected as it is discharged from the scraper and immediately after laying, this being a follow up to the inspection in the borrow area. It is easier to evaluate the character of the fill in its loose laid state broken up as it has been by its transportation, than in its naturally occurring undisturbed state in the floor of the borrow area, and this is normally the location where the quality of the fill is visually accepted or rejected. If the fill is judged unsuitable it will have to be taken up and removed, an easy though unpopular operation. If unsuitable fill continues to arrive a visit to the borrow area is required and the area may be ruled no longer acceptable. It is not common to maintain inspection continuously at both borrow pit and fill area, the latter is usually sufficient unless the character of the fill is expected to vary widely, necessitating stricter control. An excess of roots in the fill, boulders, or lenses of unsuitable cohesive material in otherwise generally uncohesive soils are examples of the cuase of rejection of fill.

Scrapers are usually routed over previously laid sections so that their passage assists in the compaction of the fill. This is normally a good practice but circumstances can occur when the pounding action of the scrapers is detrimental to the fill, in which case alternative routes should be chosen. Levelling of the loose fill by grader or bulldozer will proceed concurrently with filling. Levelling is required to spread the loose fill evenly over the area being filled and to facilitate the passage of succeeding scrapers as they run to the area being filled. This working of the fill provides another opportunity for inspecting its uniformity and for striking off pockets where fill lies too deep. With experience, the ease or otherwise of the scrapers and graders, and other vehicles, crossing loose fill can give a very good indication regarding its readiness for compaction. This is a judgement that can only be gained through experience. Having been spread and roughly levelled the fill is now ready for determination of moisture content, adjustment where necessary and compaction.

When an embankment is being built filling does not normally proceed from one end to another in one go, usually the work is divided into sections whose size is related to the length and width of the embankment and to the plant, haul distance, borrow areas, etc, available for construction. A section, say 500 m long x 50 m wide, is a commonly chosen module, the dimensions suiting the scraper runs and providing manoeuvering space for these and other vehicles. Whilst fill is being placed in one section, successive or adjacent sections will individually be checked for moisture content; compacted; and tested for compaction, density and other specified requirements. These four successive activities proceed continuously and form the basic earthworks pattern. The scene is a busy one. In the section being filled scrapers traverse continuously in their shuttle to and from the borrow area and graders are busy levelling off the fill as it is discharged from the scrapers; in the section being adjusted for moisture content graders, or tractors with disc harrows, are blading over and breaking up the fill to assist it to dry out or in readiness for spraying by water bowser where too dry and moisture content measurements are being made; the section being compacted may support a tractor and roller train trundling up and down or a self propelled compactor doing the same operation but more quickly; and lastly laboratory teams with their vehicles will be testing the compacted section for compaction and density. Just to complete the cycle, when a section has been compacted satisfactorily the scrapers move in and start laying the next layer and so the pattern repeats.

Preparation for compaction
Once a section has been filled the soil will be checked for moisture

content to see whether it lies within the moisture content range required by the specification, the requirement being quoted as the optimum moisture content plus and minus given percentages. Accurate moisture content determination in the laboratory is usually considered too lengthy a procedure to be used for the many moisture content determinations required in day to day field control and so a choice from one of the several proprietory instruments available on the market is normally employed. These instruments, sensibly used within their limitations, are a fairly satisfactory tool for control provided that they are maintained and calibrated regularly. Whatever method is employed, it is important that agreement regarding the method is reached between Contractor and Inspector. The moisture content of the fill is jointly measured in randomly chosen locations and, depending on results achieved, the fill is then either watered if too dry or allowed to dry out further if too wet. If the fill as laid is within the required moisture content range then compaction may commence straight away. Breaking up of the fill is helpful in moisture content adjustment, spraying by water bowser following the breaking up when the fill is initially too dry. Breaking up of the fill can be achieved by blading it over with a grader, harrowing it with a grader fitted with tynes or by disc harrowing. Where disc harrows are used the discs should be robust, big and heavy, otherwise they will merely ride over the fill and not penetrate it to form furrows.

It is normal practice to take the average of several moisture content values, what is important is that when approval for compaction is given the moisture content of the fill in a section is as uniform as possible and always within the specified range. Of all the parameters effecting earthworks compaction that of the correct moisture content is the most critical, if the soil is not of or close to its specified optimum moisture content then satisfactory compaction will not be achieved no matter how many passes of the compactor are made.

Compaction

Once the correct moisture content has been achieved throughout the fill, compaction is allowed to proceed, the amount of compaction having been determined in compaction trials held at an early stage of the contract. In these trials, trial sections of fill will have been laid under controlled procedures, brought to their optimum moisture content and then compacted using different combinations of rollers and numbers of passes. The combination giving the most consistently satisfactory results of compaction will be specified as the approved method to be used in the works until such times as further experience or a variation in materials will necessitate a change. Trials are intended to produce that method which requires the minimum compactive effort to achieve the specified compaction target. The approved method will stipulate the number of passes required by a given type and weight of compactor, tyre pressures for pneumatic tyred compactor, and order of compaction if two types of compactor are required. In practice the minimum number of passes is often exceeded voluntarily, a pass being defined as the number of times a single compactor, or compactor combination, passes over any given point in the fill.

Checking that the correct number of passes has been achieved is a tedious exercise if the compactor is slow moving and the area to be covered large. However, it is worth checking once or twice at least in order to ascertain how long a compactor actually takes and so be able to judge, from the time a compactor is in operation, just how conscientiously compaction has been done. Tractor towed rollers are usually slow and ungainly, taking perhaps several hours to complete a section whereas self propelled compactors can usually operate with equal facility in forward and reverse gear, are faster and more manoeuverable, and can complete the same task in a fraction of the time.

Each successive adjacent pass of the compactor should overlap the previous pass so that the area is covered completely without narrow strips of uncompacted soil being left between adjacent passes. Corners, ends and edges are the areas where compaction is most likely to be suspect, these being places where the compactors turn, line up for their next pass, or keep back from for fear of over-toppling. The situation is aggravated in confined spaces. One particularly vulnerable place is at the head of a spur where the centre of the spur head can easily be missed by the rollers as they turn, or it is churned up by scuffing wheels. In such locations the compactor may have to make a special pass, or passes, to achieve adequate compaction. Alternatively, a smaller compactor may be used in conjunction with the larger one. It is also common practice to specify proof rolling of compacted fill, that is the rolling of the compacted fill by a test roller considerably heavier than that used in the routine compaction procedure, multipliers of one and a half times or twice times being typical. The behaviour of the fill under the slow moving proof roller is carefully observed and if major defects are found they will be corrected, whereas minor defects will probably be accepted. Proof rolling is a useful acceptance test where other testing may be inappropriate or where the acceptability of fill is in dispute. The overlapping of succeeding sections is another method of achieving adequate compaction at the preceding section boundaries, the compactor running through the 'joint' before starting on its return journey. Similarly, in the case of longitudinal joints, the compactor should continue across with its passes until it has overlapped the adjacent section.

Testing

When the section is considered to have been adequately compacted, that is, that it has received the required number of passes, the Inspector will be asked to check that the required compaction, or other parameter, has been achieved. Often the Contractor will have taken his own tests as a check before requesting the Inspector's approval. Compaction tests will be taken at random in the layer and the number of tests will be related to the volume of fill placed or the area covered, and sometimes to both. The minimum rate of testing is usually stated in the specification. The locations of the tests are chosen to represent as fairly as possible the section as a whole but obviously if certain locations are thought to be suspect tests should be taken in them as well. All 'official' tests are performed jointly by the Contractor and the Inspector in the field and in their respective laboratories so as to avoid disputes as far as possible.

The depth at which the tests are taken should be determined on experience. Theoretically each section should be tested whilst it is still the top layer. The disadvantage in this is that the top layer, or at least the top 25 mm of it if the layer is nominally 300 mm thick, may be generally rather loose having been in direct contact with the wheels or rollers of the compactor. The disturbance is more pronounced when steel rollers with profiled compacting pads have been used. To overcome this effect compaction tests should be taken deep rather than shallow within the layer in question. It is also common, for the same reason, to adopt the practice of testing 'one layer down' in order to avoid surface disturbance effects.

Assuming the tests prove satisfactory, filling of the succeeding layer is then permitted. With experience it is possible to judge, with a fair degree of certainty, whether the tests on a layer will pass or fail before the full laboratory testing procedure has been completed. Awaiting the outcome of laboratory tests is not normally a bottleneck in the earthworks' programme.

The specification usually contains requirements regarding the rate of testing and also the procedure to be adopted if first tests indicate the fill to be below standard. When re-testing is required and if the second set of tests is satisfactory, the layer is approved but if these second tests give unsatisfactory results the layer is usually rejected and then has to be re-compacted. It is not necessary to take up a layer and relay it if the results of compaction tests are unsatisfactory, recompaction alone may be sufficient or the layer may have to be rescarified, adjusted for moisture content again, and recompacted. Only if a totally unsuitable layer is found is it necessary to remove it.

Apart from routine compaction testing it is sometimes required to test in depth the compaction of the embankment as a whole in which case test pits are dug, though not normally to a depth greater than say 2 m. Tests are taken concurrently with excavation and the results compared with the results achieved at the time that the various layers were compacted. It is also of interest to examine the appearance of the fill as it is exposed in the sides of the pit, check its moisture content, stratification and general soundness. Trial pits are also a useful means of investigating areas where the quality of the fill may be in some doubt, as for instance at the junction between adjacent sections.

These then, the activities of filling, preparation for compaction, compaction and testing are the basic operations of earthmoving. In the preceeding descriptions of these activities mention has been made of the various items of earthmoving plant used in these operations and now this plant is considered in some more detail, not so much in the mechanical sense but more in the sense of the performance, versatility and suitability of the different types of plant in their operation.

6 Earthmoving plant
Scrapers
There are two main types of scraper, the motor scraper and the towed scraper, the former being self propelled and the latter requiring a separate tractor unit which is usually of the track laying type. Both types have their different advantages.

Motor scrapers are by far the more common type, they come in different sizes and are fast and powerful. They can be single engined or double engined and are capable of loading themselves under their own power but are normally push loaded by one, or sometimes two, bulldozers. A special type of motor scraper called the 'self-elevating scraper' has its own built in loading mechanism and therefore possesses the advantage of being able to operate independently and efficiently without the help of push loading. The different sizes of scraper will each have their most efficient haul length and their most efficient pay load. The output of a scraper depends primarily on its speed and capacity, the haul length and the ease of loading. The capacity of a scraper may be quoted, as 'heaped' or 'struck' and some are operated with sideboards so enhancing their capacity though with some sacrifice in speed. Towed scrapers operate efficiently only over short haul distances, in the order of 200 m or so rather than over say one kilometre as for the motor scrapers. They work at a slow speed but are capable nevertheless of useful, efficient output provided that the haul distances are kept short. Towed scrapers pulled by track laying tractors can operate in soft ground where motor scrapers may founder. Towed scrapers usually operate without the need of separate tractors for push loading them.

Because they are so mobile, motor scrapers are frequently switched from section to section as the day's programme may demand. In

127

contrast, the towed scraper is best suited to steady work on short haul where it shows to best advantage. Somewhere between the two in terms of versatility and optimum haul distance lies the self-elevating scraper which combines the mobility of the motor scraper with the self loading facility of the towed scraper.

Compactors

Compactors come in a great variety of shapes and sizes and are basically of two categories, the pneumatic tyred rollers and the metal roller, the latter including smooth drum rollers vibrating rollers and those with profiled pads or feet. There is, almost, a different type of roller for each different broad classification of soil, efficient and effective compaction depending very much on the type of roller chosen and choice relying heavily on experience. By and large pneumatic tyred rollers suit more types of soil than do the metal rollers but are by no means suitable for all soil types. The pressure exerted on the soil by a compactor depends on the weight of the compactor and the imprint area of the rollers whether they be metal drum or pneumatic tyred. In the latter case tyre inflation pressures are also important as they will effect the imprint area of the tyres.

Compactor capacity should match scraper capacity. It is pointless being able to haul and spread large volumes of soil if the compactors available cannot keep up with the sections of fill as they become available for compaction. Compaction capacities usually quoted in cubic metres/hr are readily calculated knowing the speed at which the compactor travels and its effective compacting width. The coverage rate in square metres/hr is then converted to cubic metres/hr depending on the depth to which compaction is effective or the maximum layer thickness permitted by the specification. As has been mentioned earlier modern self powered compactors are fast and manoeuverable, though speed is not necessarily an advantage, and capable of high output. The familiar slow moving roller train, towed by an old track laying tractor and trundling up and down the fill is more cumbersome though it achieves the same results in the end, achieving by virtue of its greater combined dead weight what the faster compactor achieves by impact.

Graders

Of all the plant used in earthworks the grader is probably the most versatile. It is far more than just a machine for levelling roads, though this is one of its most common functions, and the calls on its services are numerous. There never seem to be sufficient graders to suit the project's demands and of all the earthmoving plant the grader is probably the most important. Check therefore the number of graders assigned to the job and try to see that they remain on duty there and are not lightly released to other sections without a good reason.

128

In earthmoving operations graders will be used for most of the following different duties, plus many more:

Maintenance of site and haul roads which includes grading, cambering and cutting of side ditches.
Levelling of loose fill as it is laid.
Breaking up the fill by the use of tyne attachments. (Check that spare tynes are available.)
Blading over the loose fill to mix and aerate it.
Trimming and striking compacted fill to the correct level and profile.

However, only in exceptional instances should a grader be employed to shift earth with its blade in the manner of a bulldozer — that is one job for which it is quite unsuitable.

Bowsers

Water bowsers are used for watering site roads and fill alike. In hot climates they assume an importance not usually encountered in the temperate climates of Europe. The best machines are purpose-built with several pressure spray points which can be controlled in motion by the driver. The simple water tanker has just one gravity spray bar, rear mounted and controlled by a hand valve which can only be adjusted when the vehicle is at rest. When bowsers are being used, check that they give as uniform a coverage as is possible for the type employed and that local flooding and hence the formation of soft spots is avoided, even if this means insisting that spray adjustments are effected away from the permanent fill. The water supply arrangements for filling the bowsers should be ample and the surrounding area well drained. There should be enough bowsers available to match the earth moving capability of the scrapers.

Tractors

Track-laying tractors are slow, powerful and capable of working over comparatively soft ground. They are used for hauling rollers or, when fitted with a blade, for push loading scrapers and general bulldozing work. To a limited extent they are used for levelling work, operating either in forward gear or in reverse by back blading, but their usefulness in this respect is limited by their slow speed and coarse controls. They may be fitted with rippers for ripping and breaking softrock or breaking up heavy, lumpy fill.

Pneumatic tyred tractors are much faster and more manoeuverable than the track-laying variety, but generally have less traction than their track-laying equivalents. The larger models make efficient compactors in their own right, sometimes their tyres are water filled to increase weight. They are seldom used to pull other rollers.

129

Disc harrows

Disc harrows are a very useful implement for breaking up and aerating the fill. To perform their job effectively they should be robust, heavy and of a suitable diameter, not less than 600 mm. Check that spare discs are available.

Dump trucks

Soft rocks like chalk, unsuitable for winning by scraper, are excavated by face shovel and loaded into dump trucks for haul to fill. Whereas scrapers appear to have reached their maximum practical capacity of about 30 cubic metres, dump trucks are still being enlarged though the larger models are restricted to site use only and even transit between sites on public roads may not be possible. In terms of payload and speed dump trucks are comparable to motor scrapers of similar rating and many of the remarks concerning motor scraper operation also apply to dump trucks. Loading facilities should match truck size and compacting facilities should match fill delivery rates. Dump trucks are suitable for longer hauls than motor scrapers.

Dump trucks are available in end tippings, side tipping and bottom dump models, the first being the most common.

Bulk excavators

Earthmoving projects which comprise essentially of mass excavation, in contrast to mass fill, for instance canal excavation or the rather more specialised open cast mining, are discussed here only briefly. The excavated material has to be disposed of, perhaps in training banks, land fill, approach embankments to structures, or dumped in stockpiles. Whatever the method, control will be required.

The excavating machinery itself is highly specialised, walking draglines or bucket wheel excavators are examples. The essence of the excavating operation lies in optimising the use of the machine to give the highest possible output — on round-the-clock operation every improvement will be significant and so will every breakdown.

Again, the output of the machine should be matched by the output of the attendant plant; scrapers and graders for making, trimming and maintaining haul roads, bulldozers for pushing the spoil into shape, compactors for use in forming the embankments and so on.

Lastly on the subject of plant, it was said at the beginning of this chapter that earthmoving plant has the habit of appearing suddenly one day and disappearing just as suddenly the next. This facility presents one of the main points which requires constant checking when supervising earthworks. Records should be kept, morning and afternoon, of the whereabouts of each individual item of major plant and any absences accounted for. Missing plant might be in for repair or might have been dispatched to open up a new section of work without prior notification to the Inspector, or it might even have left site altogether. Whatever the reason, every absence should be treated as significant and investigated.

7 Miscellaneous

Having gone through the various routine stages of earthworks operations and described the plant most commonly encountered, it now seems a convenient place to list and amplify some additional aspects of construction which frequently fall within the envelope of earthworks operations. For ease of reference these aspects are arranged alphabetically, *viz*

> Filters
> Finished profile
> Instrumentation
> Night work
> Rain
> Roots
> Stage construction
> Stoneworks
> Structures
> Survey
> Zones

Filters

What has been said for the construction of zones, see below, within the main body of earthfill also largely applies to the construction of filter layers, the latter may, in fact, be regarded as specialised zones of reduced thickness. To control the construction of filter layers, profiles or other line and thickness reference marks and gauges should be provided at frequent intervals in order that the layers may be filled to their correct thickness. Filter layers, unlike zones, are comparatively thin and therefore their depth should be checked frequently, critical points are, especially, at top and bottom of slopes and at changes of direction. The uniformity of the material within each layer should be inspected and frequent grading samples taken and tested because correct grading is of paramount importance in the specification of filter layers. Contamination of filter layer material, one layer with another or with the general fill, should also be checked and any unacceptable areas replaced.

Where filter membranes are employed, check that they are being laid strictly in accordance with the manufacturer's recommendations and also with any additional requirements which may be contained in the specification.

Finished profile

To allow for settlement and to ensure that the correct section has been constructed, embankments are usually built oversize – but not

131

grossly so. Springing from this practice, disputes have arisen regarding the extent of the compacted section required; the Contractor holding that only the cross section shown on the drawings need be compacted, the remaining outsize or overspill section being left uncompacted as laid.

Notwithstanding any requirements of the specification to the contrary, it is good practice always to compact the full cross section as laid because any loose layer will encourage erosion. Embankments must present a firm compacted face to the elements. Rain water run-off from storms, being particularly searching of soft spots, will wreak havoc in any loose surface layers at crown, slopes or toe.

Instrumentation
The amount of instrumentation built into embankments seems to be increasing each year, a tendency which as far as earthmoving operations are concerned, can only be regarded as a nuisance. It has been observed that efficient earthmoving operations depend on free uncluttered runs for all the plant involved in the preparation, laying and compaction operations. Where an instrument station is located an obstruction is formed − plant has to swerve to one side or the other to give it clearance and, because of the general sensitivity and vulnerability of such instruments and the weight of earthmoving plant, the clearance area around each instrument may be large. The particular danger is in compaction where a lens-shaped area of uncompacted fill will be left by the compactor as it keeps clear of the station. To overcome this situation the compactor will either have to make a special pass or passes to compact this area or a smaller compactor used. So, the points to guard against are the forming of pockets of loose fill around each station and damage to the installations themselves. All installations should be protected from the ingress of dirt and water and be very clearly marked at all times, especially at night if a night shift is operating.

Nightwork
Earthmoving operations frequently entail nightworking and there is generally no objection to this (third parties excepted) provided that adequate lighting is supplied and therein lies the nub. However good the artificial lighting may be, it is never as good, nor as extensive as natural daylight and this makes the visual inspection of the quality and uniformity of the fill a difficult undertaking. Where it is known that a borrow area will yield material of a generally uniform quality, nightwork presents no particular problems but where the quality of the fill is variable it is difficult to monitor satisfactorily at night and therefore best left for daytime working.

Safety precautions become an important factor for nightwork, not only for pedestrians but also for plant operators, especially drivers, who need to be controlled until they become familiar with the look of the site at night.

The commencement of a night shift entails revised or additional requirements for supervisory staff and vehicles, an aspect too often unappreciated until the last moment.

Rain

Earthworks are very susceptible to the vagaries of the weather, rain being the worst enemy. During construction, attention should constantly be paid to the ease in which the works can be protected from rain damage. Ensure that a slight cross fall is maintained in order to shed water, but if this is not practical then other means of clearing the water, for instance the cutting of temporary ditches or the provision of sumps which can be pumped out, should be considered. Newly laid loose fill is especially vulnerable to rain and, if possible, should be quickly graded over and even lightly compacted to prevent its being saturated. All plant should be kept off the earthworks until such time that the works are sufficiently dried out to support them again, premature access will do far more harm than good as the operators should know from experience better than anyone else.

Roots

If taken to the appropriate depth, top soil clearance should remove the majority of significant roots and site clearance, including the removal of trees and grubbing up of tree roots should take care of the remainder. There will always be some roots which have escaped the previous clearance operations and these are not normally of significance. The fill as laid, and excavations in the borrow area, should nevertheless be inspected for root inclusions and further action taken, such as raking by grader tynes or even hand clearance, if the inclusions be considered too widespread. A shower of rail or bowser spraying will often show up roots which would otherwise remain undetected in the fill. The walls of any excavations made in the compacted fill should be inspected for evidence of root inclusion in the fill.

Stage construction

To provide site access or to suit seasonal construction, embankments are frequently built in two or more sections. Firstly a bank of reduced cross section is constructed to provide the first season's access or protection and, later, the bank is filled to its design dimensions. When the time comes for the second stage fill to be placed against the existing section, care should be taken to ensure that the existing section is trimmed to sound fill, (the surface layers will have loosened with time), and that any accumulated construction debris is cleared away. The new fill should be thoroughly compacted into the existing fill in stepped or sloped joints to avoid a plane of weakness being formed in the fill at the plane of intersection. Where an embankment crosses a valley close attention should be paid to the construction of the connection between embankment and hill side. The drawings for these key locations will usually be finalised on site only after detailed surveys and investigations have been undertaken.

Stoneworks

Stoneworks are included here because they commonly go hand in hand with earthworks, the former provided to afford protection to the latter in the form of aprons, pitching, walls or rip-rap.

The two most important criteria for all forms of stonework are the weight of the stones individually and the requirements regarding the range of grading of the various weights of stones. Because stones cannot be as readily and frequently sampled for grading as smaller size material can be, it is useful to obtain a mental picture of the size of required weights of stone both individually and in a sample panel which has been specially prepared to suit the stone grading requirements of the specification. Both the individual samples and the panels should be maintained for comparison with the work as it progresses.

Dressed stone pitching and stone walling are both labour intensive operations, the extent of the labour content involved depending very much on the requirements of the specification regarding the dressing of the stones. However, the stability of both forms of construction rely heavily on the adequate provision of through stones which extend the full depth, or width, of the work and key it together. Stones should be placed or arranged with their longest axis perpendicular to the face of the works to achieve a well bonded arrangement. Feather-edged stones should be discarded or roughly dressed to produce a more satisfactory shape. Supervision should concentrate on achieving a good shape and weight of stone adequately bonded with key stones, an absence of feather-edged stones or stones laid flatwise, and all interstices well filled with small stones and chippings. Care should be taken to avoid damaging any underlying filters or similar graded zones during construction of the pitching. Profiles or other gauges will be required in order to achieve the correct thickness, line, level and surface tolerances stated in the specification. These dimensions should be frequently checked as dismantling stone work is a very awkward job.

The profile of any excavations required for stone aprons should be checked before dumping of the stone in the apron commences. Where the excavations extend below the water table draglines will be used to form the submerged profile and soundings will be necessary to establish that the correct section has been formed.

Filling of the apron will generally be done by dump truck or bulldozer. The correct procedure is for the truck to dump its load of stone on the surface of the advancing apron and for the stone then to be bulldozed over the edge into the apron excavation. In this way the quality of the stone, as delivered, can be readily inspected and the bulk of the dirt and small stones contained in the load will fall down into the interstices of the already filled apron, leaving only the larger stones to be dozed to fill the apron. The alternative of end dumping the truck loads directly into the excavation means that dirt and undersized stone will form part of the actual apron fill, displacing the large stones rather than filling the interstices between them.

The placing of rip-rap follows much the same principles as those just described for pitching and aprons, with inspection of the size and grading of stones and their positioning with due regard to avoiding damage to any underlying filters being the main criteria.

If the quality of stone as delivered is outside the specification limits the stones should be rejected and representations made to the quarry to bring the stone to the desired standard. Check that rejected stone really is rejected, not returned later by the same truck. Control may be achieved by noting lorry numbers and journey times.

Structures
Filling and compacting against such structures as retaining walls and bridge abutments or against and over included structures such as access, drainage or service culverts should be carefully controlled or damage will be caused by collision or displacement to the structure by the action of the heavy plant. Special care and attention is also required because, as large scale operations cannot be used in these locations, haste may overcome prudence and the fill may be deposited in an excessive loose depth resulting in its subsequent inadequate compaction. Restrictions are usually placed on the approach of heavy plant to structures and so, within the area immediately adjacent to the structure, compaction by hand operated plant will probably be necessary. There are, in any case, bound to be awkward corners, around buttresses, drawpits and the like where hand compaction is the only possible means. Check that any waterproof membranes provided for the structure are not damaged or displaced during backfill operations and that drainage filters, weep holes, joint forming materials, and other similar provisions are maintained to the full design requirements.

Survey
Survey plays a key role in all earthmoving operations. All bench marks, profiles, and monuments should be checked and cross checked regularly. All such reference points should be clearly marked so that

identification is easy; in a featureless countryside it is all too easy to make a mistake in the value of the reference points being used simply because they all look alike. Further, they should where possible be located at suitable offsets clear of the works and protected to minimise the risk of their being damaged by traffic. They should be marked conspicuously by beacons or similar signs so that future location is made simple — what might appear to be at the time of installation a well marked location often proves to be very difficult to find the following day.

During construction check that the dimensions of the earthworks at any given stage are correct, eg bed widths, side slopes, and widths for any given height.

Zones

Embankments may not be homogeneous but, instead, may embody a zone or zones, of material different from that of the main body of fill. If this is the case, and it is a common design feature, not only will variations in the filling and compacting procedures be required but also attention is necessary to ensure that the zones are constructed to the correct profile and in the correct locations within the bank. The extent of each zone should be clearly marked by profiles or other setting-out devices which will require regular checking and adjusting as the embankment rises. Areas to watch particularly are at any changes in direction or section and at the commencement and curtailment of the zones. In practice the zone boundaries will not form a clean sharp line as indicated on the drawings but zone interfaces should be maintained as true and correct as possible and minimum dimensions should be maintained at all times. The specification should contain placing tolerances which are appropriate to the plant to be used for construction, if tolerances are not originally specified they should be determined and agreed before work proceeds.

Another point to check is that contamination of zones is kept to a minimum. Some boundary contamination will be inevitable, but with care appropriate to the degree of cleanliness required, zone contamination can be reduced to insignificance in the core of the zone. Common methods of achieving this are constant grading and striking, maintaining a difference in levels between the adjacent materials, clean access roads and run-on areas, cleaning of plant, especially tyres, and the provision of separate plant for constructing the zone. Samples of zone material should be taken frequently for grading and other characteristic analysis as it is most important that zone material meets the requirements of the specification.

8 Specialist Construction

In this chapter the supervision of works requiring specialised techniques is discussed. A selected list of items has been chosen and these are as follows:

Chimneys (concrete and brick)
Concrete folded plates and shells
Cooling towers
Demolition
Diaphragm walls
Dredging to reclamation
Electrical plant installation
Explosives
Ground compaction by vibrating probes
Instrumentation
Marine blockwork gravity walls
Masts and towers
⚡Mechanical plant installation
Old structures
Post-tensioned concrete
Railways (permanent way)
Rubble mound breakwaters
Shaft sinking
Shoring and underpinning
Site investigations
Sliding shutters (slip forms)
Steel bridges (major)
Tubewell and wellpoint de-watering
Tunnelling
Underwater work by divers

Although this book is concerned primarily with the general principles and practices of supervision rather than with the supervision of particular subjects, the inclusion of these examples will illustrate the application of these principles and practices in a variety of fields. Whatever the speciality, guidance and direction should be sought from, and given by, senior and experienced staff working in conjunction with the requirements of the specification. Statutory health and safety regulations will govern procedures in many operations, eg in mining, tunnelling and diving, but they are not included here under the separate items.

The supervision necessary for the specialist items described in this

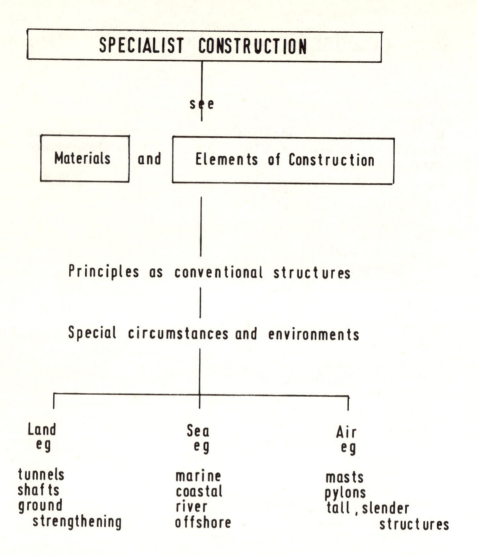

SPECIALIST CONSTRUCTION

see

| Materials | and | Elements of Construction |

Principles as conventional structures

Special circumstances and environments

Land eg	Sea eg	Air eg
tunnels	marine	masts
shafts	coastal	pylons
ground	river	tall, slender
strengthening	offshore	structures

Diagram 8

chapter should be considered as being additional to the supervision required as part of normal construction routine.

The items are now discussed in alphabetical order.

Chimneys (concrete or brick)

Whatever its construction, a chimney should be plumb and true throughout its length, any deviation will be all too apparent to the naked eye.

Whether plumb is controlled by plumb wire or by optical means, and a plumb wire is always preferable though not always practicable, a constant check should be kept on the verticality of the structure.

With tapered chimneys, taper, height and wall thickness are all related and should be correlated each against the others.

Check also for signs of twist, skew or wander by comparing the chimney profile and top centre point with external vertical reference lines (eg a line thrown up by theodolite).

Check that the chimney is correctly orientated with respect to the flues it serves and that all openings for flues and access have been correctly provided and positioned.

If temporary guy wires are used, see that they are correctly tensioned at all times, neither too slack nor too tight.

If the chimney is lined, ensure in good time that provision is being made for the supporting nibs or corbels.

For the lining, check the bonding if brick, tie-backs or other fastenings to the outer shell and, if prefabricated, the joints between successive lining panels.

Check that all fastenings and built-in items are provided and correctly positioned, eg fixings for steeplejack ladders, aircraft warning lights, lightning conductors.

Check the completed height of the chimney.

Concrete folded plates and shells

In the construction of these members it is most important to erect the formwork as accurately as possible in accordance with the geometry of the drawings so that the relationships used in the design are reproduced faithfully in the structure.

Ensure that the formwork and its supports are adequate to resist, especially, the horizontal and torsional forces that will be imposed on them by the nature of the structure. The end and edge supports to the plates and shells require particular attention in this respect.

Check that all reinforcement has been placed correctly. It may not be obvious by eye, and from experience with conventional structures, whether the reinforcement has been placed in the positions required by the design, always check the reinforcement bar by bar against the drawings.

Because sections are usually comparatively thin and where top shutters are used, the cover to bars, the securing of bars (or mesh), and the vibration of the concrete should be most carefully controlled.

Cooling towers

Although the shell of a reinforced concrete natural draft cooling tower is its most obvious feature, the foundations and the columns supporting the shell are substantial elements and all should be considered acting as a whole in the construction of the tower.

Perhaps more so than with other structures, setting out is done from the centre point for all elements and so the centre point should be repeatedly checked from start of foundations to topping out. Numerous reference points should be established outside the tower so that the centre point can be re-established if lost during construction.

Raising the centre point is conveniently done by a plumb line in a dash pot, backed up by regular theodolite checks.

Check that foundations, ground beams, plinths and columns are all structurally integrated and pay particular attention to the positioning and making of construction joints.

A substantial pattern of piling is probably required by the design, check that all piles have been driven and are subsequently picked up in the later stages of construction.

Check that the columns supporting the shell are correctly aligned, they usually form a vee pattern and are usually raked to suit the slope of the shell.

Check, and have independently checked, the required diameter at each level. This is important for each lift of the shell.

Measure the thickness of the shell. Ensure that the correct pattern, spacing and type of reinforcement is being used and that changes are made at the required levels. Because reinforcement is fixed in a regular rectangular pattern particular attention is necessary on this matter.

As with chimneys and other tall isolated structures, ensure that all built-in items and inserts are located correctly and securely.

Check that door openings and starter bars for nibs and corbels are not forgotten.

Because of the relatively thin section of the shell, care should be taken when locating these items after casting the shell.

Demolition

A demolition job may be beset with such constraints as to make the job more a case of dismantling than the image generally associated with the term demolition, or the job may be quite free from constraints in which case the work proceeds in the rather vigorous manner of general demolition. Whichever may be the case, it is necessary for the demolition contractor to propose a sequence of working which, when approved, should be strictly followed.

The following observations apply mainly to the case of structures requiring 'controlled' demolition rather than 'uncontrolled' work. Both terms are relative, no demolition will be completely uncontrolled and all or some of the following common methods may be employed:

explosives	chain and ball
deliberate collapse	thermic lancing
jack hammer	by hand

The structure to be demolished should be carefully inspected together with all relevant drawings and design.

The structural system should be determined and note made of such construction details as joints, bonding, bearings, etc.

Any existing services should be located and dealt with.

Note that prestressed work generally and ungrouted tendons or bars in particular, need special attention. Consult the original design in such cases.

Note that the thrust from arches may need to be contained temporarily at some stage during their demolition.

Remember that controlled demolition will follow very closely the reverse sequence of construction, ie removal of dead load, then spanning members, then supports. A knowledge of the structure is thus essential and modern buildings with complex structural patterns and stringent codes may prove more difficult to demolish than older and perhaps structurally simpler buildings.

Diaphragm walls

This section discusses the construction of concrete diaphragm walls by the bentonite slurry displacement method.

This form of construction has the disadvantage that the work cannot really be inspected in progress because it is all submerged in the slurry. Inspection is only possible on completion when the ground adjacent to the walls has been excavated.

To ensure that the completed work is satisfactory the trenches for the walls should be accurately set out and constantly checked for width, depth, and plumb.

The reinforcement cages should be checked to see that they are correct and capable of being handled without distorting when being lowered into the slurry filled trenches. Placing should be done carefully to avoid disturbing the trench sides.

The concrete mix should be suitable for placing by tremie and care should be taken not to displace the reinforcement during concreting operations.

The bentonite slurry should be checked for quality and consistency from time to time to ensure that it remains capable of supporting the trench sides and produces a clean job in that reinforcement and concrete are not adversely affected by dirty slurry.

When excavating the earth between completed walls ensure that all necessary bracing is provided and that the designed depth of excavation is not exceeded. During these operations the alignment of the walls should be monitored in order to reveal any movement.

Dredging to reclamation

Although the procedure of dredging to reclamation may not seem to be a very active operation, very large volumes of material are involved and the item is commonly one of the largest and most expensive in any major marine work's bill of quantities. In supervising the operation, the following matters which relate to cutter-suction dredging a navigable channel and reclaiming a nearby area for development, require attention. The remarks are, however, generally applicable to other dredging/reclamation operations.

A joint agreed survey of the area to be dredged and the area to be reclaimed is necessary before the work commences and after the work has been completed.

A sequence of working should be agreed. The Contractor should submit, for approval, cut plans showing dredging cut and reclamation sequence with setting out points.

It is particularly important that the 'as-dredged' survey is most comprehensive in order to minimise the risk of undetected high spots on which ships could ground.

It is usual to 'sweep' areas dredged for navigation purposes as positive confirmation that no high spots remain between survey lines. This is done by towing along closely-spaced transit lines an apparatus, usually built up on site and known as a 'sweep' and consisting of a steel bar set to the dredged level, attached to a frame the top of which can be seen above water. Hence any snagging of the bar on a high spot is immediately detected and buoyed.

When dredging close to structures much care should be taken to keep to the designed depths in order to avoid undermining the structures. Backfilling may be required if the overcutting is beyond tolerance.

The dredger's position should be carefully checked to ensure that the correct areas are being dredged. Radio and radar positioning devices are commonly employed though sextants are still used for small schemes.

The depth of dredging, side slopes and widths of channels should be checked during operations.

Records should be kept relating volumes and areas of dredging to volumes and areas of reclamation. Boundaries should be as well defined as possible. The depositing of fill may well be selective, the poorer material being specified for unimportant areas and the better material required for areas intended for priority development.

The characteristics of the dredged material should be regularly determined and compared with the information obtained at the initial site investigation survey. Any indications of the presence of rock or other hard material are particularly significant as these materials profoundly affect the rate of dredging.

Check that the drainage facilities at the reclaimed areas can cope with the rate of delivery of the dredged material.

It is essential that close attention is paid to the frequent extension and/or movement of the point of discharge and the path of the return water, in order to minimise segregation of the dredged material. This is usually done by pumping into discrete bunded areas; even so, the Contractor should be persuaded to move the discharge point as frequently as possible.

The keeping of records is a most important part of the task of supervising dredging operations. The following list includes the major items which need recording daily:

Time to mobilise the dredger and its pipelines or barges
Working hours and downtime
Type and number of all plant used both afloat and ashore
The size of all equipment, diameters of suction and delivery pipes
Types of cutter head used and length of times each is in use
Length of delivery pipes and points of discharge
All movements of the dredger and its cutting pattern
Sea and weather conditions
Time spent moving pipes
Barge journey times and number of journeys.

Modern dredgers carry sophisticated instrumentation by which their performance is controlled. If practical the readings from these instruments should be recorded, by direct observation if print-out is not available.

Measurement of the volume of material dredged may be by (a) survey of the dredged area, or (b) survey of the filled area with due allowance for ground settlement and bulking of the fill, or (c) by dipstick in the barge hoppers. Method (a) is the most common for dredging/reclamation schemes.

Electrical plant installation

What has been said about the installation of mechanical plant applies equally to the installation of electrical plant. (See the later section on mechanical plant installation, page 148.)

If one item of electrical plant were to be singled out as being more vulnerable to site damage than any other it would be electrical cables.

The position of buried cables should be plotted and conspicuously indicated by surface markers. The depth to the cables should be shown on plan and marker posts. Cables buried in the soft, ie direct in the ground, are especially vulnerable. Tiles, tape or ducting provide some protection whilst ducting surrounded by concrete provides good protection. The position of cable joints, if joints are allowed, should be recorded.

Check that the correct type of cable is being used.

Explosives

The use of explosives in assisting construction is one of those operations that really is best left to the expert. The Inspector's main role, as far as general site blasting is concerned, will be in ensuring that damage is not caused to other parts of the temporary or permanent works or to adjacent property, and that all the necessary safety precautions have been followed and the appropriate authorities notified.

The supervision of quarry blasting is normally related to controlling the size and/or quality of the stone being supplied. It will also be necessary to check the quarry output for payment purposes.

The size of stone required will dictate the type of explosive used. Large blocks, for monumental masonry or breakwater construction for example, will need a slow burning, heaving action, low explosive whereas small stone for use as roadstone or concrete aggregate requires a detonating high explosive. The explosives used in rock tunnelling are of the latter type, the small stone produced being convenient to muck out.

Misfires are more commonly caused by faulty circuitry (or damp powder in cord fuses) than by faulty detonators and explosives.

The common aim where explosives are regularly used as a routine part of the works is to achieve the maximum quantity of the right sized stone with the minimum quantity of explosive. This is a matter of finding the correct combination of drilling pattern, sequence of firing, weight and type of explosive for the rock type being blasted and can only be achieved through experience and by trial and error.

Ground compaction by vibrating probes

The process is used for non-cohesive soils. Spacing of the probes will be determined in trials until the specified density compaction has been achieved, these parameters are usually checked by the Standard Penetration Test.

It is convenient to establish a regular pattern of probes when covering the area to be compacted. All probes should be to the depth required by the specification, a point to be noted during inspection.

The crater formed by the probe will be filled with non-cohesive soil of the specified grading, the grading of the soil used should be checked regularly.

In order to obtain a measure of the effectiveness and uniformity of the treatment the quantity of soil required to fill each crater should be measured. The time taken for each probe insertion and withdrawal should be controlled until the optimum period is found.

As in the use of other mechanical devices constant checks should be made on the mechanical operation of the probe and notes made of all the instrument readings, to ensure that the machine is operating in the most effective fashion for the ground being treated. The rate of vibration, for example, should always be checked and also the power delivered to the probe.

Check that probes of the approved type, length, diameter and mechanical specification are being used and note their serial numbers to assist identification.

Instrumentation

The instrumentation of major structures as an integral part of the course of their construction has become a common practice.

Instruments are usually expensive, delicate and sophisticated requiring careful handling and secure storage prior to installation.

To obtain maximum benefit from them, instruments should be installed accurately and securely and their positions carefully recorded.

Instrument positions should be clearly marked during and after construction to reduce the risk of their being damaged.

The instruments should be regularly checked during construction to see that they have not sustained damage. If they have, the sooner this is discovered the better in order that repairs may be made.

In many instances instruments are installed at the very beginning of construction in order to record parameters during construction. It is also common for the construction itself to be controlled by the readings obtained from the instruments, the readings being compared with the original design assumptions. This is particularly common in earth and rockfill dam construction.

Certain structures, such as flumes and weirs, are measuring devices in their own right and should be constructed to very close tolerances and finishes if accurate readings are to be obtained from them.

Marine blockwork gravity walls

Although the blocks, nowadays generally of concrete, used in marine blockwork wall construction are very large they still need to be manufactured and positioned to a high degree of accuracy.

Erection should be carefully controlled to ensure that the desired profile of wall is maintained, and that the wall remains stable at all stages of construction.

The two major criteria in gravity wall construction are the stability of the structure and its resistance to slip. These criteria apply to all levels, not just at the base. Construction and supervision should therefore be undertaken with these points always in mind.

Vertical and horizontal joints between blocks should be to the required tolerances and bond pattern.

Check that all mechanical connections between blocks are provided as required by the design and that they are properly made.

Check that all provisions for drainage have been made. Any selected granular backfill behind quay walls should be checked for grading and profile.

Backfilling behind the walls should be carried out strictly in accordance with the agreed procedure.

Service ducts or galleries within the wall should maintain alignment from block to block.

The wall should be closely monitored for settlement during and after construction.

Thorough underwater survey and control is essential in ensuring a sound bed and foundation for the wall. The alignment, stability and level of the foundations should be carefully checked not only at commencement of construction, but also regularly as construction proceeds. The need for protection, or additional protection, of the foundations from erosion needs special attention at all times.

A very close watch should be kept on foundation excavation. Samples of the excavated material should be examined as frequently as possible, and a programme of sampling and testing, eg penetration tests, established with the contractor, to check that design assumptions are valid.

No site investigation is ever as good as the construction process and this is especially true of underwater work.

Diver work will almost certainly be required for all the underwater work. This should proceed to a pre-arranged programme with checks on all significant items (see also the section on Underwater work page 158).

The difficulty is that the work cannot be seen except by divers, and frequently not even by them, hence tight surface control on setting out and the working procedure is vital.

Always keep a weather eye open. As part of Records, the following information should be recorded daily at all marine sites:

Wind speed and direction.
Wave height and direction.
Local currents (if possible).
Times and heights of High and Low Water.

Such observations do not necessitate complicated recording instruments, simple observations are quite sufficient provided that they are done conscientiously. It is the period over which such observations are made which is important and significant, not so much any scientific niceties in recording techniques.

Masts and towers

These structures, because of their specialist nature, may fall outside the scope of the British Standards relevant to more conventional structures. In the case of repetition work, eg electricity transmission towers, it is often economically justifiable to test one tower to destruction in order to verify design assumptions and to prove construction techniques, but for one-off structures, such as television transmitter masts, such a full scale test is unlikely. In both instances construction procedures should pay full regard to any limitations imposed on them by the designers.

The structures fall into two broad categories, the free standing types and the stayed types. The former are generally assembled piece by piece on site whilst the latter are usually delivered to site in pre-assembled sections of convenient length for site erection.

Because of the comparatively slender proportions of the members construction should be carefully controlled and due attention paid to maintaining the structure in a stable condition at all times.

Check that all necessary bracing, both temporary and permanent, is provided horizontally, vertically and diagonally.

Check that stay wires, temporary or permanent, are provided at the correct intervals and are correctly tensioned. Uneven tension forces will impose undesirable torsional loads on the structure.

All members should be checked to see that they are not bowed, bent or otherwise damaged or distorted before, during and on completion of construction.

Lack of straightness in struts will cause significant weaknesses as will any damage to stay wires.

Check that any necessary packing is provided at joints and intersections.

During erection provision may have to be made to allow for temperature or wind induced stresses, and a continuous check should be kept on the plumb and/or taper of the structure.

Foundations and anchors should be checked for structural integrity, position and orientation. Check that the structure is being erected to the correct orientation.

Where a pad foundation forms the base of a free standing mast the soil beneath the base and the backfill surrounding it should be thoroughly compacted. Any tilting of the base will throw the super structure immediately and obviously out of plumb.

Free standing steel floodlight high masts are usually delivered to site in sections for assembly. During assembly check that the seams of the sections are in alignment and that the correct force is applied in pulling one section on to the next.

Corrosion protection systems, galvanising or paintwork, should be most carefully inspected and any damage made good to the requirements of the specification.

In transmission line work, ensure that the correct type of tower, suspension, corner or anchor, is being constructed at each tower site.

Mechanical plant installation

The installation of mechanical plant is an extensive, complex subject in its own right and here only the very barest guidelines can be listed.

Many items are special orders on long delivery so when they arrive on site see that they are handled carefully and stored safely prior to installation.

Their installation frequently requires a clean environment. Special provisions may be necessary before installation can commence, and after installation is complete, to protect the plant from general site dust and debris.

Installation tolerances are usually fine, requiring patient, careful setting up and checking before and after final fixings.

Ensure that openings left for the installation of plant are large enough to accept the plant.

Carefully check the positions and strength of holding down bolts and other fastenings provided for locating and securing the plant.

Pay particular attention to statutory testing procedures for all lifting appliances, eg cranes, lifts, hoists, ropes and cables.

The separate and distinct requirements of commissioning testing and acceptance testing should be identified and their respective procedures clearly defined. The former may be considered as the setting in motion of a stationary system and acceptance by the Contractor of the system from the manufacturer; the latter, the testing of the system to the requirements of the specification for acceptance by the Inspector from the Contractor.

The resulst of all tests should be carefully recorded and agreed.

Old structures

In renovating or converting old structures, in whole or in part, one of the main problems may be that there are few, if any, existing drawings, let alone calculations, describing the original structure. If this happens to be the case a thorough survey of the structure should be undertaken before new work is commenced.

Another likely drawback is that there may have been little or no maintenance of the structure, especially in the more recent years, and this should be borne in mind when undertaking any survey.

Some or all of the following examinations may be necessary:

Excavate trial pits to inspect the foundations or footings.

Inspect basements for damp, cracking or deflections.

Check walls and corners for plumb, square, cracking or bowing.

Inspect the roof structure for soundness and to see if it is water-proof.

Check areas where beams and slabs take bearing and the sufficiency of the bearings.

Check the state of all structural members, not forgetting any tie rods, and their connections.

Determine which way beams and slabs span and follow the loads to the foundations, ie determine the structural system of the building.

Pay particular attention to any previous modifications to the original structure.

Check the state and layouts of all existing services, eg electrical wiring, water mains and internal plumbing, drains, gas, chimney flues and chimney stacks, guttering and rain water pipes.

Take a look at the condition of any adjacent buildings to see how they are fareing.

Make sure that every aspect of the new survey is accurately and permanently recorded for future reference.

Post-tensioned concrete

Although, quite rightly, the emphasis in prestressed work is on the quality of the prestressing appliances themselves it must not be forgotten that all the other elements involved also need to be of a very high quality. All the usual inspections necessary in reinforced concrete work are also necessary in prestressed work besides the inspections required for the prestressing assemblies.

Quality control of the high strength concrete should be strict. The formwork should be accurate, all dimensions should be checked carefully. Check that all the conventional reinforcement is present and accurately positioned, especially at the anchorages.

The anchorages, being highly stressed, need particular checking in all respects. Often anchor blocks are precast for later incorporation in the *in-situ* pour of main members. In such cases the positioning of the anchor blocks should be checked carefully, particularly for the security and squareness of the fixing within the main shutters.

Check that tendon bearing plates at the anchorages bear correctly against the concrete.

Check that the tendon profile for each tendon is correct and that the correct number of tendons is present.

Check that the correct tendons are actually being used, each tendon should bear its own identifying label.

149

Check that the correct sequence of stressing is followed.

In determining the elongation required for each tendon, ensure that the particular elastic modulus and stress-strain curve, for each particular tendon is used in the calculations.

Before tendons are inserted in ducts, ensure that the ducts are clear of grout runs, kinks and any other obstructions. Joints in ducts should be securely taped or otherwise jointed to keep the ducts clear of grout ingress.

Where the tendons and ducts are grouted up after stressing ensure that the grout used is of the correct mix, including any additions, and that it is freshly mixed. Take care to verify that grouting is complete throughout the duct length.

Prestressing tendons, unless galvanised wire is used, are particularly sensitive to corrosion so each tendon should be carefully inspected for any signs of corrosion before it is approved for use.

All splices in prestressing wires should be most carefully examined, be in sound working order and be used strictly in accordance with their manufacturer's recommendations. Gauges used in measuring prestressing force need careful calibration.

Wire, or rod, extensions produced should be checked and compared with the prestressing force shown on the gauges.

If precast beams are to be partially prestressed for moving from their beds in the precast yard, check that they are of the required age and strength and that the partial stressing force is correct.

Check that camber is correct at all stages.

Railways (permanent way)

In Great Britain permanent way works are nowadays confined largely to the maintenance and improvement of existing tracks though from time to time comprehensive upgrading of selected routes is undertaken. Where completely new track, as opposed to track improvements, has been laid in recent years it has been virtually all in marshalling yards and sidings or as private industrial line and not as main line work.

This is not always the case in other countries and the following remarks may be taken as being applicable to all permanent way works.

The control of earthworks in cutting or embankment will follow normal earthworks procedure.

Particular attention should be paid to the arrangements for drainage.

The alignment of the track, gauge, curves, super-elevation and general setting out should be carefully checked.

Check that the ballast conforms with the specification, is clean, and is sufficient in width and depth.

Inspect all sleepers, concrete, steel or timber, to see that they are in good repair.

Inspect all rail/sleeper fastenings to see that they are secure, complete, in good repair and are of the appropriate type for the rail/sleeper combination in question.

All rail should be inspected for cracks, splits, wear and other defects whether the rail be in the standard sixty foot lengths or in continuous welded rail. Defective rail should be replaced and all defects reported. Details of the rail are carried in various letters on each rail so that each individual rail is fully identifiable.

Check all welded connections in continuously welded rail and check that anchor lengths are correctly fastened.

Check the bolted fish plate connections between standard rail lengths and inspect the bolt holes for signs of incipient cracking.

Switches, crossings and other mechanisms with their associated controls should be inspected and tested to ensure that they are all in good working order.

Ensure that the specified minimum clearances are maintained between the track and trackside structures, eg to bridges, signal columns, platforms, tunnel faces.

When working on existing lines maintain very close liaison with the railway authorities. All track possessions should be carefully scheduled and require careful preplanning.

When carrying out maintenance inspections the bridges and other structures, platforms, embankments and cutting slopes, drainage, water courses and all elements making up the permanent way should be checked.

Rubble mound breakwaters

The construction of a rubble mound breakwater may appear to be a rather coarse procedure devoid of much engineering skill. In fact, as is the case with many seemingly unskilled operations, a good deal of care and attention is required if the structure is to succeed.

In the construction of rubble mound breakwaters the three important items to check are the side slopes, the weight and grading of the rock forming the armour, and the shape of the armour rock. The first two items are key parameters in the design of the breakwater and the third is important for achieving a satisfactory interlock between the individual armour stones. In this section primary armour is described as rock armour. It may also however be of concrete units, the same general criteria apply to both types. Prior to construction, the establishment of setting out reference points is necessary in order first to locate and then to control construction.

The grading and quality of the hearting stone should be regularly checked at the quarry and as delivered to site.

The size and shape of the armour rock should be regularly inspected

151

at the quarry and as delivered to site. (For control of stone works see also the section on Stoneworks page 134.)

Underwater survey and inspection will be required to ensure that stones are being deposited in accordance with the profile shown on the drawings.

Check that currents are not removing or displacing the stone as it is being deposited. Hearting stone is particularly vulnerable to displacement being lighter than rock armour. Ensure that all depressions or hollows are satisfactorily filled and that the hearting is brought up evenly. The hearting is usually deposited by bottom dump barges or by end tipping dump trucks.

In zoned construction ensure that each zone is correctly located and built to the correct slopes with the correct sized stone. Check all leading dimensions of each zone.

Check that rock armour is laid to the correct thicknesses on slopes and crest. Underwater slopes may be checked by hand soundings, not by echo sounder. Slopes above water are checked by profile boards. Check each layer before the next is placed.

Check that the rocks of the armouring are placed to form a well knit interlocking layer with broken joints and no thin flat faces. The armouring should be placed, not simply tipped without further adjustment. Secondary armour is usually tipped and then trimmed. Primary armour is placed by crane, each stone being placed individually and its position recorded.

Ensure, that as far as possible, the works are constructed in sequence which leaves no part vulnerable to storm damage, armouring should closely follow hearting.

Check that all plant operates from a stable position. This is important for its own safety's sake and also for achieving accurate work, eg placing armour rock.

Shaft sinking

An essential feature of mining engineering, shaft sinking is also widely encountered in civil engineering in conjunction with tunnelling works.

The following matters appertaining to vertical shafts require particular attention:

The ground strata passed through should be continuously observed for signs of faults, deterioration, changes, water bearing seams, etc.

The verticality of the shaft should be constantly checked.

The shaft dimensions should be checked to ensure that the shaft is running true and is not being displaced or distorted.

All framing and bracing should be regularly inspected for signs of distress under load. Check all connections.

The condition of structural members should be inspected for signs of rot, rust or corrosion as the case may be.

All ground water met should be regularly analysed as it may contain corrosive elements which would attack both temporary and permanent works alike. Concrete, bricks and mortar are all susceptible to ground water attack so ensure that the correct types of each material are being used.

It is essential that all mechanical gear be regularly inspected and maintained, eg ventilation, services, communications, cages, brakes, lifts, cables and winding gear.

Ground freezing is widely used in conjunction with shaft sinking. In this method particular attention should be paid to the following items:

The alignment and verticality of the bore holes containing the freezing liquid should be checked to ensure they are sunk clear of the permanent works.

The temperature and thickness of the shell of frozen ground should be constantly checked, both down the sides and at the bottom of the excavation. Inspect the lining and base for signs of thawing.

During excavation care should be taken to avoid cracking the surrounding ice wall of frozen ground.

Check that no item of the permanent or temporary construction is adversely affected by the freezing conditions.

Shoring and underpinning

Before commencing shoring or under-pinning works, a knowledge of the structural framing and load layout of the structure to be treated is essential.

Inspect the existing structure and note its condition especially any weaknesses or points of potential weakness. These inspections should be done jointly with the owner or his representative as well as with the Contractor. Such inspections should be done regularly, not just at the beginning and end of operations.

Particular attention should be paid to old buildings which will usually be weaker than more modern ones and whose records may well be unavailable. Local strengthening, propping and bracing may be required.

Establish datum points in the structure so that its behaviour can be monitored for signs of distress.

In positioning shores check the following:

Raking shores require a good sound bearing both horizontally and vertically at their upper and lower ends.

In placing flying shores ensure that the support reaction can be safely contained by the restraining support.

Check that all wedges, bracings, props, bearings, etc, are securely fixed and cannot slip.

All shores should be braced to safely resist buckling and torsion.

153

Check that the shore foundations are clear of the permanent works or, if this is not possible, that satisfactory alternative provisions have been made to overcome the problem.

In under-pinning work, apart from normal structural considerations ensure that:

All equipment is reliable. Gauges and other load measuring devices employed are calibrated and working well.

Every practicable precaution has been taken to avoid or minimise differential settlement.

All excavations are adequately shored and braced to prevent unintentional under mining (which will almost certainly lead to differential settlement).

Site investigations

Although site investigations are frequently carried out by specialist contractors (or sub-contractors) employing specialised equipment it is still necessary for their work to be supervised by someone who has a good knowledge of the work involved. The supervision of site investigations is a skilled job and requires a knowledge of standard site investigation tests and procedures, the parameters being investigated and at least a general description of the type of structure intended to be built.

Site investigations should proceed according to an approved plan showing the location where major investigation is required, in as great a detail as possible, and to an approved programme of execution.

During supervision attention should be paid to the following:

In executing the tests and recording the information great attention should be paid to detail if the full benefit of the tests is to be obtained.

The investigations themselves should be carried out conscientiously and, in the case of standard tests, in accordance with standard procedures.

Inspect the equipment supplied, see that it is correct, complete and in good working order.

Apart from the specified records obtained from the tests the Inspector should make his own notes of any items he considers significant. These notes frequently provide invaluable background information to the data recorded with the tests.

Visual observation of adjacent ground and the type of terrain may reveal useful additional information. Inspect such items as existing wells, water courses and quarries.

Enquire if previous investigations have been made and study all existing records and the history of the site. The locations and extent of any existing pits, shafts or mine workings should be thoroughly investigated.

Check that the location and ground level of each individual test is recorded accurately.

Check that all samples are identified labelled, packed and stored securely and despatched as necessary.

Negative results or 'failed' tests will be as significant as positive successful tests and should receive the same amount of attention.

Large boreholes and most test pits will probably require back-filling, see that they are.

Sliding shutters (slip forms)

In construction using sliding shutters, pre-planning is absolutely essential.

Construction proceeds non-stop on a twenty-four-hour-day system so shifts, supervision, transport, etc, should be suitably organised.

If work has to stop for any unscheduled reason, it is necessary to unstick the shutters from time to time by slight movement to prevent them adhering fast to the setting concrete.

Plumb, orientation, absence from skew, etc, should be regularly checked.

Check that all items needed in construction, especially built-in items, are available before the slide starts.

The supply of cement and fine and coarse aggregate should be checked to ensure sufficient is available, especially over weekends and public holidays.

Standby plant should be available in case of major breakdowns, and repair facilities for the minor ones.

If ready mixed concrete is being used, ensure that the supplier is organised for weekend and public holiday working.

Some means of direct communication, telephone or W/T, should be provided between ground and shutters, notes will not always be suitable as the intervening distance increases.

The hoist or tower crane used for access and transport of materials should be checked/serviced each day.

Any boxouts in the shutters should be easily removable after casting-in, plywood is difficult to remove.

All boxouts and built-in items should be securely and accurately fixed. Boxouts should be easy to locate after casting but small inserts, eg steeplejack ladder fastenings and aircraft warning light fixings can be very difficult to find. The method of fixing built-in items should be proved before construction starts.

Reduced levels should be taken up the slide to ensure all items are located at their correct level. This is conveniently effected by providing a purpose made gauge running the full height of the slide with reduced levels, insert levels and all other significant items marked on.

Steel bridges (major)

The subject of the construction of major steel bridges is so specialised that only brief mention of some of the many important aspects can hope to be mentioned here. Perhaps the most important concept to grasp is the inter-dependence the different elements have one on another and that construction is very much more than a simple matter of bolting everything together. To assist in the essential task of visualising in three dimensions the relationships of the structural elements it is a good idea to construct simple models in cardboard or balsa wood to represent the structure in question.

Separate matters requiring particular attention are as follows:

Bearings should be inspected to see that they have been installed correctly and have the necessary clearances — are they upside down or incorrectly orientated for instance? Is their material condition satisfactory, especially rubber or synthetic rubber components?

The grade of steel being used may require special electrodes and welding techniques, check that the correct material and procedures are being used.

Check that expansion joints are unobstructed and free to move.

Check that all cambers have been correctly set or achieved.

Temporary supports, bracing, etc, will play a major part in the construction of most bridges, therefore ensure that the concept of erection is clear to all the members of the Contractor's and Inspector's staff who are involved. Check and double check before altering or removing any falsework, jacks or other items of temporary works.

Ensure that all temporary construction expedients are made good at completion. Such expedients include lifting holes, access holes, drainage provisions, etc. Where such making good is necessary check that remedial painting is executed to the full appropriate specification.

Check that construction is kept within the allowable tolerances for all items. A certain amount of lack of fit is almost inevitable but if tolerances are exceeded remedial measures should be most carefully and thoroughly examined before being approved. Such attention should be paid to minor and major members alike, it is frequently the minor items which cause the most problems.

Keep the whole bridge structure under observation, not just the portion under construction. Ensure that the bridge is adequately protected from collision damage during (and after) construction.

In composite construction check that the shear connectors are correctly welded to the steel beam flanges and that the flanges have not been damaged in the welding process.

Tubewell and wellpoint de-watering

Deep de-watering may be achieved by submerged pumps operating in tubewells and shallower de-watering by wellpoints operated by surface pumps.

In both systems the grading of the filter material used and the condition of the filter cloths should be checked. If the filter material is contaminated or the filter cloth torn replacement is necessary.

Filter material should be sealed at ground level to prevent air being drawn down into the system through the filter.

Water levels in tube wells and any other monitoring points should be read daily.

A means of measuring the quantity of water discharged from a de-watering system should be devised if practicable.

Discharge channels should be inspected regularly and any erosion, damage, or obstruction put right.

Pipe joints on the suction side of a wellpoint system should be checked for tightness.

Check the number of pumps in use, their state of repair, and if standby pumps are available.

Check that standby power is reasonably readily available in case of major fault in the prime system.

During construction inspect the condition of the bottom and the sides of the excavation for signs of trouble in the shape of boiling or sloughing.

Existing nearby structures may be affected by ground settlements caused by the pumping zone of influence so inspect the structures and the ground they stand on regularly.

Tunnelling

First and foremost, the setting out should be done to great accuracy and checked several times over. Major tunnels of several kilometers length are perforce often set out from the bottom of access shafts, giving a base line length of say 20 m at the most.

Accurate setting out is necessary not only for the obvious reason of driving the tunnel to the correct line and level but also so that the position of the tunnel in relation to its surroundings is known.

Clearances should be maintained between any existing known structures, services, ground level or hazardous ground and depth of cover maintained under rivers and sea bed. The latter is especially important when compressed air is being used in the tunnels, insufficient cover could result in a blow-out occurring.

Note that whereas hydrostatic pressure is greater at the bottom of the tunnel face than at the top, the air pressure required to resist the hydrostatic pressure is uniform and equal to the maximum hydrostatic pressure, resulting in an excess outward pressure at the top. It is this excess pressure which often causes blowouts at the tunnel top.

The quality of the ground being passed through should be continuously checked so that precautions may be taken in good time if the quality of the ground is seen to be deteriorating. This is especially important in compressed air tunnelling where ground quality will determine the amount of air required. Every effort should be made to obtain information concerning ground conditions, not only from the usual extensive site investigation contract but also from any available existing local records.

In soft ground the plumb of access shafts should be frequently checked. Tunnels in soft ground should be checked against distortion by measuring horizontal and vertical diameters at each segment ring.

The reliability of the setting out should be matched by the reliability of all the mechanical plant utilised in driving the tunnel, in fact setting out and mechanical plant may be considered as the two key aspects of tunnel driving. Regular inspection and servicing should be given to the cutting machine or shield, the mucking out train, lights, drainage and ventilation plant. In a compressed air tunnel the air compressor and air locks also need regular inspection.

Where used, segmental linings, usually of precast concrete or cast iron, should be accurately positioned to the correct diameter. Bolting, caulking and sealing of the rings should be thoroughly done.

Where *in-situ* concrete linings are used, ensure that the concrete completely fills the forms. This may be difficult in the upper portion and crown of the tunnel especially if reinforcement is present.

The annular space between lining and earth face should be grouted up.

All types of lining may need supporting temporarily until the complete linings are under sufficient external pressure to develop the lining's strength, otherwise the linings may distort or deflect temporarily.

Where the tunnel is formed by drilling and blasting check that overbreak is not excessive.

Underwater work by divers

The following remarks apply particularly to construction in relatively shallow water within the range of compressed air diving techniques rather than to deep sea works.

Request details of the divers' training qualifications, experience and grading.

Insist on a first class survey before construction starts. Supervision of the survey should be monitored from the surface and diving done only to check on specific points.

Many common construction activities are fundamentally the same underwater as on land with the same matters requiring attention.

On any job working methods should be simplified and standardised as far as possible in accordance with the principles and limitations of underwater work for the common benefit of construction and inspection.

Collect and study all available existing surveys and records, the more information gained before work starts the better.

Tide gauges should be established as soon as possible, also survey data for line and level. Care, patience and ingenuity are required in transferring survey datums from the surface to the sea bed. Such data once established should be robust and easily located.

Underwater visibility and currents restrict thepace and fineness of tolerance of construction. Much work is done by touch and therefore construction, especially connections, should be simple and tolerances ample.

Due allowance should be made for refraction.

Whenever possible work should be programmed to afford maximum protection to divers and the work in hand from currents, eddies, etc. Divers' shifts are normally restricted to four hours maximum duration because of fatigue limits.

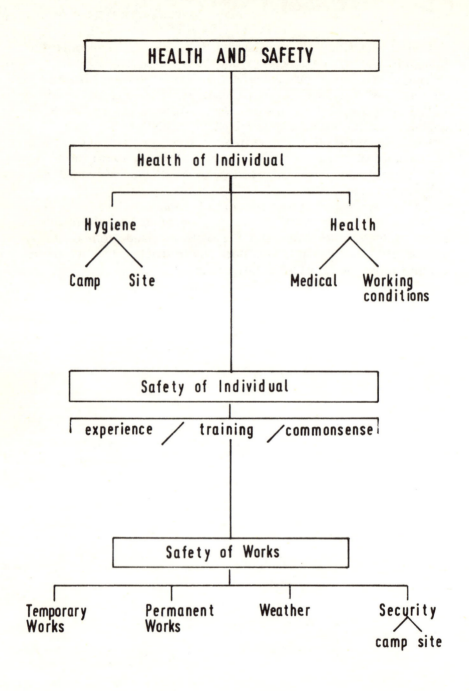

Diagram 9

160

9 Health and Safety

The principles and practices which go towards the upholding of good standards of health and safety on construction sites are very much the same as those necessary elsewhere. Education and training, the observance of established procedures, common sense, and persistence are all essential in maintaining a safe and healthy site.

In this chapter the two broad headings of Health and Safety as they relate to the health and safety of the individual and to the safety of the works are discussed under the separate sections:

1 Site hygiene
2 Health
3 Personal safety
4 Temporary works
5 Permanent works
6 Weather.

The last may seem an unusual inclusion but adverse weather can seriously affect the safety of the works under construction or partially complete, especially the safety of marine works and tall structures. The chapter concludes with a brief section
7 Security.

The construction industry as a whole does not have a good health and safety record though, with increasing effective legislation, this record is improving and the days of lip service only to safety precautions are largely gone. By its very nature the industry encompasses occupations and materials which cannot be free of a certain element of risk but the risks can be minimised by exercising control and attention and avoiding foolhardiness; there is unfortunately still too much of the latter about. Certain elementary safety precautions like the wearing of safety boots and safety hats are obvious and usually obligatory. Others, like the spotting, avoidance (and correction) of 'traps' in scaffolding can, perhaps, only be learned through experience. In health, medicine is revealing hazards perhaps suspected but not recognised a few years ago, indeed the continuing introduction of so many new construction materials is bringing with it the introduction of new hazards.

When a fatal accident occurs on site the site may close down for the remainder of that day, or longer, and the effect on site morale is depressing. On a large site the affect of a death of a person largely unknown to the majority of the work force may be impersonal, but it is felt nevertheless. On a small site a death is felt very keenly.

If a major accident results in many deaths then the outcome on site may be very serious indeed. Strikes may occur, the site may be forced to close, investigations and legal proceedings are bound to arise. (These may all, of course, occur after one fatality, they most certainly will in the case of many fatalities.)

Education and training are necessary in order that the lessons learned from past experience may be passed on to as many persons as possible and also to keep up to date with current findings. Most sites now have a safety officer, if not a safety committee, with responsibilities that include the displaying of posters and the arrangement of lectures and films on health and safety matters. For maximum impact the posters should be simple and explicit, for maximum interest the lectures and films should be relevant to the works on site. There are also numerous publications available which describe, seriously and light-heartedly, in one manner or another the various hazards met with in construction.

Education may be said to help reduce accidents in two ways. Firstly, by helping construction to be planned in such a way that hazardous situations are avoided and, secondly, by helping to ensure that any existing, potentially hazardous situation is recognised and rendered safe before it causes an accident. Experience, though important, cannot teach everything and takes time to acquire.

Rather like some specifications, standard procedures are written in the light of past experience and current knowledge. Their purpose is to define and regulate methods of operation so that only methods known to be safe are followed. Certain types of construction, like compressed air tunnelling, mining, and diving, are strictly prescribed by procedures laid down in legislation. Examples of current legislation are The Factories Act, The Health and Safety at Work Act, Diving Operations Regulations, Building Regulations, Mines and Quarries Act. The Health and Safety Executive has administrative and investigatory powers. Other aspects of construction procedures do not have such weighty authority behind them but are drawn up by individuals or by committees at site level, for instance by a site safety committee, to govern particular operations on site. Examples of these operations are the overhead erection of large precast elements or the use of explosives in pipe line excavations through rock. The agreed procedures are often issued in the form of a check list with the items listed in the desired sequence. The procedures do not have to be complicated to be effective, in fact the simpler they can be made the better will they be understood and remembered.

The use of procedures is necessary in some cases to ensure that not only do the operatives follow the correct sequence but also that others working nearby know what is going to happen. To take blasting as an example again, the sequence of warning sirens and flags should be made known to all in the adjacent areas, not just to the operatives themselves.

Many procedures may appear to the newcomer to be cumbersome and unnecessary. Whilst improvements and simplifications are always welcome, short cuts should never be taken in ignorance.

Lastly, on the subject of procedures mention should be made of emergency procedures. Most permanent places of work, offices, factories and the like, have standard emergency procedures which are displayed on notice boards and which are practised from time to time. Such arrangements are uncommon on construction sites but contingency plans to deal with site emergencies are very much worth while, going beyond the simple expedient of phoning for public emergency services. On remote sites public emergency services may simply not be available as a practicable emergency service in which case the site does have to be well prepared to deal with emergencies independently.

Most site accidents are a result of carelessness, accidents to a person because of his own carelessness or accidents to one person because of another person's carelessness. Most site accidents, too, are simple ones which occur also in every walk of life and could so easily be avoided. Persons working on site for the first time should not think that different safety rules apply on site compared with say, city life. The same basic rules apply and the same common accidents do, unfortunately, occur.

Commonsense should tell a person to look where he is going and where he is putting his feet, to look out for site traffic (especially motor scrapers) to stand in shelter if overhead work is progressing, to avoid standing on the edge of excavations not only to avoid falling in but also to avoid dislodging objects onto those working in the excavation. The trouble starts when commonsense is ignored for the sake of expediency or for reasons of bravado. There may be apparently good reasons why short cuts are made at the expense of certain safety measures in order to get a job finished quickly but the reasons have to be very good ones before such action could be justified.

There is certainly no excuse for bravado but unfortunately there is much of it about; scaffolders are probably the worst offenders together with structural steelwork erectors. It is agreed that they need a cool head for heights and that confidence comes with practice but familiarity too often leads to over confidence and carelessness. Motor scraper drivers on their fast and powerful machines are also often guilty of exhibitionism, perhaps understandable but dangerous nevertheless.

A few posters stuck around the site and a film show once a year are not going to do much in the way of raising the general level of site safety consciousness, nor is one week's vigorous campaigning. To make a whole site safety conscious for the duration of the contract needs an organised, sustained safety programme from start to finish of the job and a trained safety officer with appropriate authority. On small sites there will probably be just one safety officer, provided by the Contractor. On large sites, employing several contractors, there will probably be a chief safety officer provided by the main contractor and a safety committee representing the other contractors and the Inspector(s). Because of pressure of work on senior staff it is often the more junior staff members who get assigned to the safety committee. This is beneficial in as far as it provides good experience for them but has the disadvantage that they often do not have the individual authority to affect decisions on site.

A continuous contract-long programme of posters, lectures and films, and the display of the site safety record is required to help keep a site safety conscious all the time but these, the psychological media, are not in themselves sufficient. For effective health and safety control all Inspectors should keep a look out during their daily rounds for hazards and have them corrected. Some obvious examples are open manholes, unguarded edges or holes of suspended slabs, projecting scaffolding, unguarded lifts and hoists. It should not be thought that once corrected the same hazards will not recur, more often than not they will recur the following week if not the following day. Scaffolding guarding an opening will be taken for another purpose; timber boarding over a hole will be used for shuttering; warning lights may be knocked down or stolen; all will need reinstating, and persistence is required to see that they are.

1 Site hygiene

A large project in a remote area in a hot climate will need to organise its hygiene arrangements very carefully. The Contractor's offices, workshops, staff camp and labour camp and the Inspector's offices, and staff camp will all need water supply, washing facilities, toilets and drainage. Of these establishments, the labour camp will be the largest. There will also be a need for kitchens for the offices and the camps, again the labour camp being the largest. There might be a laundry, there probably will be fresh food shops or stalls and a bakery. All these facilities could, if not maintained satisfactorily, present a threat to good site hygiene and should, therefore, be subject to inspection and control. If the control cannot be exercised by a local authority, perhaps because there isn't one, then the responsibility usually devolves upon the main Contractor. It has been explained already that each site usually has its safety officer and, similarly, residential sites will also have a health officer, usually the Contractor's camp doctor operating from the camp clinic or hospital.

The precautions to ensure good hygiene are well known, here are a few:

Check the incoming water supply system to see that its mechanical parts, ie, pipes, pumps, valves, joints boreholes, etc, are sound and not cracked. Sample and test all water supplies regularly. Ensure that drains and channels are working freely and are not blocked.

Stagnant water should be drained and prevented from reforming.

Check that the foul sewage drainage and disposal system is functioning correctly.

All kitchen waste should be burned. External domestic water tanks should be covered.

Foul soakaways should not be located within the vicinity of water supply boreholes.

The location of toilets should be carefully chosen.

Vermin should be exterminated.

Domestic animals (pets excepted) should be controlled if not banned.

'Camp follower' shops supplying the camp should be subject to the camp regulations for health and hygiene.

Satisfactory health certificates are required for those workers engaged in the installation of water supplies.

The above remarks reflect requirements in an extreme example and obviously will not all apply to all projects everywhere. The availability of local public utilities, like water supply or drainage, is an advantage if these utilities are reliable. A point to remember is that, although the hygiene and health regulations of other countries may be equal to those in Great Britain their standards of application and control may be inferior.

2   Health

Mention was made in the previous section on Hygiene of a camp clinic or hospital. The extent of the medical facilities provided on site will depend on the size of the project and where the project is situated. In a remote area a large project with residential camps will have its own field hospital for construction personnel and their families and a first aid clinic at the site itself. The hospital will have a full medical staff and be equipped to deal with common ailments and injuries and also with births, of which there will be more than a few, and deaths, of which unfortunately, there may be one or two. Such a site will usually have its own site ambulance. A small site, by contrast, may have simply a first aid clinic and attendant to deal with minor injuries, anything more serious being taken care of by the local hospital.

The giving of prophylactic injections and vaccinations is a continuous activity for clinics in countries where such measures are recommended, or obligatory, to conform with local health regulations.

Probably the most obvious and visible hazard to health on a construction site is dust of which there are numerous kinds, some more harmful than others. Dust is not the only common health hazard though, there are many others which may be conveniently grouped under the separate headings of Chemicals, Fumes and Gases, and these four groups will now be considered briefly in turn. Within each group a list of the main offending materials or elements is given, together with an indication of how their associated hazards may be reduced or eliminated. A fifth group Miscellaneous is also included. The Inspector should always be alert to these hazards because they are present, either obviously or potentially, on all construction sites. He should see that action is taken to eliminate the hazards as far as possible and that appropriate site first aid and rescue facilities are always available, and in good working order, to deal with emergencies immediately they arise, eg drench showers, fire fighting equipment, stretchers.

Dust

General site dust, aggravated in excavations and mining
Asbestos in all its many forms
Glass fibre materials, especially when applied by spray
Silicon, the most notorious of all
Cements, limes and plasters
Pulverised fuel ash
Sawdust and wood shavings

Controlled by damping, natural or mechanical ventilation, avoidance of working by sawing or drilling.

Chemicals

Paints of all descriptions, lead paint in particular
Adhesives
Solvents
Lubricants
Bituminous products, pitch and tar
Acids and alkalis

Controlled by ventilation, storing in conditions recommended by their manufacturers.

Fumes

Solvents
Welding, electrodes may contain dangerous chemicals
Gas cutting, especially galvanised metal

Controlled by ventilation.

Gases

Carbon monoxide, from combustion
Hydrogen sulphide, found in sewers

166

Nitrogen dioxide, produced by welding
Carbon dioxide
Inert gases, eg argon, halon can cause asphyxiation
Gases may give rise to both poisonous and explosive atmospheres

Controlled by ventilation, respirators may be necessary and also indicators.

Miscellaneous
X-rays used for checking welds and other units for structural integrity.
Ultra violet and *infra red rays* as used in welding arc lamps.
Lasers, commonly used in setting out tunnels.
Noise and *vibration* anywhere.
Fire, although always a major threat, does not in fact occur as often as might be expected. This is surprising in view of the many combustible items always present on site, eg fuels, paints, timber, plastics.

When a fire does occur on site it is usually the programme that suffers most of all, damage to stores and plant on long order usually being the casualities. Major sites, especially petro-chemical sites, may have their own auxiliary fire appliances to provide an immediate fire fighting facility.

In chapter 3 Materials, a selection of common construction materials was discussed with respect to their correct use on site. As a means of showing where and how health hazards may arise on site these materials are now considered again in the context of this present section. For convenience the injuries most commonly caused by the respective materials are also listed.

Steel reinforcement:	burns from gas cutting gear: injuries to fingers.
Cement:	dust hazard, whether stored in silos or bagged; also burns.
Sands and aggregates:	silica dust if materials are very dry.
Pipes:	burns from jointing solvents; injuries to fingers and toes.
The laboratory:	burns and fumes from miscellaneous chemicals: injuries to fingers and eyes from materials under mechanical test.
Quarry and crushing plant:	silica dust, explosives: injuries caused by falling stones and stones thrown by blasting.
Lime and plaster:	dust and burn hazards.
Batching plant:	combination of hazards found with cement, sands and aggregates.

167

Contractors stores:	chemicals, solvents, paints; all may give rise to hazardous fumes, and fire is a general hazard.
Timber:	sawdust and shavings as well as general fire hazard: woodworking machinery, eg bandsaws, circular saws, and planers, is dangerous and needs skilful operatives.
Structural steelwork:	hazards from welding fumes and paint systems: injuries caused by falling objects, eg bolts and tools, and by falls from elevated work.
Clay bricks:	some dust hazard.
Blacktop:	hazards from fumes, and solvents: chemical burns are common, also burns to the soles of the feet caused by walking over newly laid hot materials.

3 Personal safety

Safety sense is a combination of common sense, training and experience and the newcomer to site will no doubt have the first commodity, a little of the second and, by definition, none of the third. Because training is based on the experiences of others it is hoped that the following remarks will augment training already received, leaving experience, which can only be gained personally.

A code for personal safety on site is, rather like the highway code, a list of do's and don'ts, simple to appreciate but dangerous to ignore. Unfortunately, carelessness and laziness, rather than inexperience, are the two main causes of site accidents as statistics, of which there are many, will indicate.

The following is a short collection of precautionary examples which, if not heeded, commonly give rise to accidents. More comprehensive lists are easily obtainable and are usually included in the many books and booklets published on the specific subject of safety in construction. The Inspector and Contractor alike should become well acquainted with such information and should endeavour to ensure that all persons working on site, and visiting, do so likewise; indeed the visitor is probably more vulnerable than the site worker.

Always wear safety boots and safety helmets, even for the shortest tour of inspection or site visit. Helmets should be obligatory. See that spares are available for the use of visitors.

On a large site don't wander across unfamiliar areas of the site where work is, or has been, progressing, so running the risk of unknown or unappreciated hazards, eg excavations, haul routes, partly buried work, electricity cables, buried or overhead.

Similarly, don't take short cuts through other Contractors' working areas, this could be unwelcome as well as dangerous. Men working in confined excavations are always at risk and should be safeguarded by all practical means. Keep onlookers, stores, plant and spoil away from the edge of the excavation; ensure that exits are unobstructed at all times; carefully inspect side supports; carefully inspect the condition of the ground in the side of the excavation and along the top perimeter for signs of deterioration, subsidence, movement on bedding planes in rock, etc.

Give right of way to construction plant, especially earthmoving plant, unless at controlled crossings and even there be careful.

Don't follow closely behind earthmoving plant, many vehicles can and do travel as fast in reverse gear as they can in forward gear.

Men are quite justified in refusing to work in conditions which they consider to be unsafe.

Keep clear of overhead work unless the area is well protected. This may appear obvious within buildings but is easily overlooked externally where over head conveyors, cables and such like may be under erection.

Don't stand immediately beneath the edge of overhead slabs, stand either in the protection of the slab or well clear of its edge to be safe from objects falling off the slab's edge. The scaffold tube met end on at forehead level is a common danger all too easy to overlook until too late.

Check the clearance beneath overhead cables before moving plant, especially cranes. Height profiles should be provided at all crossings. Temporary access ramps sited (badly) beneath such cables may reduce overhead clearances to below the recommended minimum.

Erect and maintain warning notices as appropriate. In the construction of tall structures, eg chimneys or television towers, remember that those who have worked on the structure from the beginning will have become accustomed to the height whereas newcomers, unused to working at a height, may be unsteady for a while.

During night work don't rely on being seen in the light from site lighting, carry a torch and wear reflective clothing. Develop the facility of looking forward and downward simultaneously in order to avoid walking into obstructions, tripping over them or falling down them.

Mechanical plant and machinery require particular safeguards; for example screening to such moving parts, as pulleys, belt drives, cables and counterweights, and the ducting away of exhaust fumes.

Electricity and items of electrical plant present their own particular hazards which are just as potent in temporary installations as they are in permanent ones.

Frequently the commissioning of one section of work involves the use of one or more other sections still undergoing completion inspections. Personnel engaged on the respective duties of commissioning and inspection should make absolutely certain, by checking with the commissioning/inspecting personnel responsible, that all sections involved are clear and safe before embarking on their respective procedures. Examples are the commissioning/inspection of aircraft runways, cooling water culverts, and sea outfalls.

4   Temporary works

The previous sections on hygiene, health and safety were discussed as they related to personnel on site. This section on temporary works and the two following on permanent works and weather respectively are discussed as they relate to the safety of the works.

Temporary works may be defined as including all works of a temporary kind required for the construction, completion and maintenance of the works, the term 'works' itself being taken to include both temporary and permanent works.

Permanent works means those works to be constructed, completed ana maintained in accordance with the contract. For convenience construction plant is discussed in this section on temporary works though in usual construction definitions it is considered as a separate matter. Permanent plant is however normally included within the definition of permanent works.

When inspecting temporary works the onus of responsibility should be clearly understood and appreciated, this is vital. In assessing this responsibility there are three principles which are distinct and yet interrelated, each should be considered and not one overlooked. Firstly, under normal contract conditions, for example those of the Institution of Civil Engineers, responsibility for the design and construction of temporary works rests firmly with the Contractor. The Inspector should be careful not to attract this responsibility to himself unintentionally. Secondly, the Inspector does have a responsibility towards his Client to ensure that the temporary works are satisfactory, will serve their purpose and will not be detrimental to the progress of the works through inadequate concept or design. If the job is delayed through inadequate temporary works the Client suffers.

Thirdly, is the wider issue that everyone who has a direct supervisory position on site and who is competent to make appropriate judgements has a responsibility. Should the Inspector be aware that the temporary works are inadequate, and a failure occurs, the Inspector may well share responsibility with the Contractor.

The subsequent observations in this section should be read with the above principles in mind.

Temporary works are as varied in form and scope as permanent works, ranging from simple structures taking a day or two to complete, for example simple scaffolding or pipe culverts, to extensive complex works taking months to prepare, for example, cofferdams required for marine works or for river diversions in hydro works. Where work is dictated by seasons a whole year may well pass before any significant permanent works are commenced, the time being taken in completing the preceeding temporary works. Whatever the scale of the works, the principles of good construction still apply and works should be soundly constructed and have structural integrity, discrete and overall. Although the life of temporary works is shorter than the life of permanent works and the stringent design criteria applied to the latter may be inappropriate and unnecessary for the former, it is quite possible that extreme loading conditions may occur during the life of temporary works which should be anticipated and for which due provision should be made. Where temporary works directly support permanent works then the safety of the permanent works during construction will depend entirely on the adequacy of the temporary works. Shortcomings in the latter may put the former at risk and may not always be obvious at the time of construction. This is especially true in ground drainage and earth works.

The consequences of failure in temporary works may be no more than a nuisance, perhaps only to the Contractor if the failure involves, say only part of his workyard or camp, but may be a catastrophe if major permanent works are also involved, as in a bridge span collapse or a cofferdam failure.

It is a common requirement for details of design, by way of calculations and drawings of major temporary works, to be submitted by the Contractor to the Inspector for checking. This procedure does not relieve the Contractor of his responsibilities but does provide a further check on the safety, suitability and practicability of the temporary works. For certain specialist structures the Inspector may deem it necessary to design the temporary works himself, thus assuming the responsibility for them.

The construction of key temporary works should be monitored and recorded, with regular inspections appropriate to the materials and elements of construction being used. The basic materials, eg steel, cement and timber, used in the temporary works will be the same as those used in the permanent works whereas the elements of construction most commonly used in temporary works, eg scaffolding, formwork, soldiers and walings, although following the same general principles as are found in permanent works, are largely peculiar to temporary works.

However, it is not uncommon for certain temporary works to be incorporated in later permanent construction in which case their standards of construction should be equal to those required for the

171

permanent works; steel sheet piling is one example.

When inspecting temporary works the Inspector should draw the Contractor's attention to any apparent weaknesses. The Inspector's attitude should be helpful, critical in a constructive manner when necessary, and should not be scornful or superior when failures are encountered. Often much more is to be learned from one failure than from many successes, by Contractor and Inspector alike. Temporary works should be kept under constant surveillance both during their construction and in use when their construction is complete. Look for signs of distress which may be occasioned by the design loadings, by unanticipated loading conditions or by improper use of the works themselves, this last is a frequent fault. As a corollary, guard against the improper or unsafe use of permanent works as temporary support for other works under construction, eg for anchoring stay wires, providing reaction support to formwork or simply as storage space for building materials.

Some of the more common elements of construction used in temporary works are now discussed with regard to what to check during inspection.

Scaffolding   The apparent maze of a scaffolding cage should resolve itself, with study, into a repetitive pattern. Look for a pattern, if there is one the scaffolding is probably well constructed. If there is not one but just a hotch potch of tubes in all directions, the scaffolding might be immensely strong or might be very unstable. Check that:

The verticals are firmly founded, with shoes as necessary, and that any packing is securely fastened.

Adequate longitudinal, transverse, diagonal and cross bracing is provided.

The scaffolding is regularly and securely tied into existing works where this is possible or, where the scaffolding is self supporting, that it forms a continuous, tied, self bracing structure.

Toe boards, handrails and planks are all securely fastened and seesaws or traps avoided.

Warning notices, barriers and lamps are provided at the base of the scaffolding.

Mobile scaffolding   Apart from considerations of stability the main danger is from unsecured items such as planks, tools or pots of paint falling off the scaffold when it is being moved — it is all too easy to start moving the scaffold before checking overhead first.

Grillages   A grillage of steel beams is a common foundation for heavy temporary works. The weak points are the beam webs which should be stiffened.

Falsework   Heavy steel falsework should be checked for; adequacy of bases with stiffeners as necessary, correctly made connections with welds, rivets or bolts all present as required; correctly provided stiffening in beams and columns; correctly provided diaphragms and bracing. Many proprietory systems of support are available on the market; bailey bridging is an example of one of the heavier duty kind.

Cofferdams   Steel sheet pile cofferdams should be checked for:
Alignment and maintenance of alignment whether curved or straight.
Clutch interlock.
Adequacy of cross, ring or other forms of bracing and strutting.
The ground conditions at foundation level.

Earthen cofferdams should be checked for:
Settlement
Slope stability and erosion
Toe stability

Formwork   The arrangement of panels, soldiers, walings, struts, props and ties which together form a system of formwork should be examined individually and collectively for strength and stability. Check the formwork by following the loads to the ground, member by member, connection by connection, from shutter face to foundation. Fastenings and connections should be made securely.
   Props and struts should be well braced.
   Ties should be securely anchored.

Materials generally   Many of the materials used for the construction of temporary works will not be new, frequently they will have been used several times before on different sites for different contracts. They may, or may not, have been refurbished in the Contractor's general yard before being sent on to a new contract. Their condition should be checked and repairs or replacements made as necessary.
   Compressed air hoses, couplings and tools require careful handling and so too do all tools which utilise an explosive device.

5   Permanent works
In this section the safety of completed items of permanent work is considered with respect to the damage each is most likely to sustain, or to which hazard each is most vulnerable. The causes of damage are simply listed against each item. The items are chosen from those discussed in chapter 4 Elements of Construction, regarded as individual items, and in chapter 8 Specialist Construction, regarded as complete structures.

Elements

Arches, domes and vaults
Subsidence of abutments or springings.

Beams
Insufficient end bearing.
Over toppling, especially edge and parapet beams.
Impact from tall vehicles.

Blacktop construction
Solvent spillage
Settlement of backfill to underlying services.
Sympathetic cracking in line with shallow buried structures.
Tracked vehicles.

Brickwork and blockwork
Uneven settlement of footings.
Restrained thermal movements.

Buried services
Insufficient top cover resulting in crushing or displacement by surface loads.
Badly marked, resulting in their being dug-up during later excavations.

Cantilevers
Impact by vehicles driven to the building line and not noticing the cantilever.

Cement bound granular materials
Uneven settlement and undermining.
Thermal movements impeded by soffit restraint.
Unauthorised traffic.

Columns
Impact by vehicles, not only on the column but also on its base.

Concrete paving
Restrained thermal movements at soffit, joints and adjacent structures.
Tracked vehicles.
Spalling of joint edges.

Drains
Uneven settlement caused by over excavation and inadequate compaction of backfill.
Underlying hard points from poor bedding material.
Insufficient top cover to surface loadings such as traffic or stored items.

Electrical and mechanical plant
Handling during unloading, storage, and installation. General site dust and weather if stored out of doors.
Fire in the case of electrical plant.

Fencing
Vandalism.
Bank slippage or subsidence.

Handrailing, walkways, etc
Impact by construction plant.
Incorrectly used as anchors for stay wires, etc.
Dismantled for access and not re-erected.

Kerbs and paving slabs.
General damage by vehicles scraping against or driving over.
Disfigurement by bituminous sprays.

Masonry
Fair faces scratched, edges and corners chipped.

Mounted services
Restrained thermal movements.
Falling items, eg dropped tools, flooring panels.

Paintwork, tanking, plastics, glass, plaster works, ie general finishes
Dropped items, general site hazards.
Sunlight, hot sun may cause plastic panels to distort.

Precast items
General handling and stacking.
Badly made or damaged joints will cause instability.

Retaining walls
Displacement by earth moving plant, especially at expansion joint locations.

Roofing
Safe loads exceeded when used for unauthorised storage or access.

Secondary steelwork
Impact by construction plant.

Simple bridges
Expansion joint fittings and nosings broken by traffic and stones wedged in joint gaps.

Slabs
Overloading by temporary construction, stored materials.

Stairs
Chipped nosings, scored soffits.

Structures
When inspecting completed structures look especially for:

Chimneys
Plumb, cracked linings, distress at joints (concrete, steel or brick-work).

Cooling towers
Cracks or distortions in the shell, cracks in ring beam at and between supports.

175

De-watering
Fluctuating water levels and discharge.
Diaphragm walls
Bowing and bulging, movements at toe.
Marine walls
Subsidence, deviation from line, bulging, movement at joints.
Masts and towers
Plumb, bowing, twisting, slack or over-taut stay wires, distress at bases.
Permanent way
Subsidence, cracked sleepers and rails, incorrect gauge, bad ballast.
Rubble breakwaters
Subsidence, disturbance of armour, overtopping.
Shafts
Plumb, bulging, general distortion in shape.
Shells and plates
Cracks in span and edge beams.
Tunnels
Distortions in shape, obstructions to clearway, cracks in concrete, brick or segmental linings.
Under pinning
Signs of crushing, settlement, undermining, distress in mechanical parts, eg jacks.

6   The weather

Construction, being almost exclusively an outdoors activity, is very much at the mercy of the elements, the degree of vulnerability depending to a large extent on the location of the site and the type of work being undertaken. As a class, at one end of the scale, marine works are probably the most vulnerable whilst, at the other extreme, could be small building works inland with a large proportion of the work completed under cover, (permanent or temporary). Unseasonal or unexpectedly severe weather can and does delay construction work beyond the period that could be allowed as being reasonably foreseeable, causing construction programmes to be extended. In countries where weather is distinctly seasonal, for instance in the monsoon belt, or where extremes of temperature are experienced, construction will be programmed to best match the seasons.

Weather imposed loading conditions, eg from wind, snow and waves, of what may be called normal predicted severity are taken into account at the design stage of a structure and these loads are generally sufficient to ensure appropriate structural stability. The forces and vagaries of nature being as they are however, abnormally severe or freak conditions, eg tidal waves, tornados, cloudbursts, or combinations of conditions do occur which may cause extensive damage or failure in parts or in the whole of the works and against which it is neither practicable nor realistic to design. The best safeguard in these circumstances is often reliance on thoroughly sound construction and integrity of the structure in question. Such integrity may not be enough to prevent significant damage but is often sufficient to avoid immediate catastrophic collapse and consequent loss of life — building in earthquake zones are designed with this philosophy in mind. It should be made known from the outset if a structure embodies unique design features to particularly resist natural conditions and close control is imperative to ensure that such features are built correctly.

The remainder of this section deals with what may be termed normal expected adverse weather conditions and the bearing they have on the safety of the works as well as on more general site considerations.

The discussion follows the order of prediction, action before, action during, and action after storms. But first some remarks on some manifestations of adverse weather.

Dust storms
   Reduce visibility to a few metres.
   Block drains, affect mechanical and electrical plant.
Extremes of temperature
   Affect site mixed materials which set and gain strength chemcially.
   Plastics are also affected.
Ice
   This builds up on overhead lines and lattice structures.
Lightning
   Masts and other tall structures at risk.
Rain
   Rail will soon reveal any inadequacies in temporary and permanent drainage.
Snow
   Its weight is easily underestimated.
Wind
   Material blowing about the site is dangerous; high waves at sea.

Although nothing can be done about the weather as it happens, a good deal can be done to find out what weather may be expected at a site and to take precautionary measures if the forecast is bad. In Great Britain, general and regional weather forecasts are available from the Meteorological Office, radio and television, and the telephone service, whilst more detailed local forecasts may be obtained from local radio and television services, airports and harbours, and forces establishments.

Examples of common precautionary measures normally taken in the event of predicted storms are as follows:

Temporary grading of earthworks to shed water.

Checking, or cutting, of temporary drainage ditches.

Checking of stay wires on towers and masts.

Securing of tower cranes on their rails with the jibs usually left free to rotate.

Erecting of temporary bracing to partially erected and hence possibly vulnerable frameworks.

Weighting down of sheeting material, eg asbestos cement, corrugated steel, or plywood. Such items blowing over a site can be lethal.

Withdrawal of plant from exposed positions, eg cranes from breakwaters.

Postponement of scheduled operations, eg long concrete pours, beam lifts.

During a storm the whole of the works should be kept under observation however unpleasant or uncomfortable a job this might be, as far as it is safe to do so, each section being responsible for its own works. It may be found necessary or even vital to strengthen defences in some quarters if the original ones are seen to be inadequate or are feared to be so. It is also important that records are made of the storm and its effects, as accurately as possible under the circumstances.

As soon as possible after the storm, the whole of the works should be thoroughly inspected for signs of damage and for signs of any inadequacies in the design of the works. Common examples of storm damage are the undermining of foundations, erosion of banks, flooding, dislodgement of stone protection, blowing down of columns, tearing of lightweight cladding or roofing, and the failure of fixings. All damage, whether to temporary or permanent works, plant or materials should be recorded and photographed as too should any signs of inadequate design. Examples of the latter may be drainage culverts too small, stone protection too light, bracings too slender, banks too steep or too low. Damage and design short comings should be reported to Head Office.

7 Security

Responsibility for the security of the works, and for the camps if there are any, usually rests with the Contractor and it will be his duty to make the necessary arrangements in liaison with the local authorities. In certain countries security is a significant part of labour organisation and control, in camp and in works. The following remarks relate to site security only.

The easiest site to make secure is a self contained one where the minimum requirements of a fence and a controlled exit are all that are necessary. By contrast some sites, say a motorway, canal or coast protection, are almost impossible to secure as far as control of access by unauthorised persons is concerned.

Common security arrangements include fencing, controlled access through manned gates or barriers, vehicle passes and personnel passes. The Inspector's staff are duty bound to conform to all reasonable security arrangements made by the Contractor.

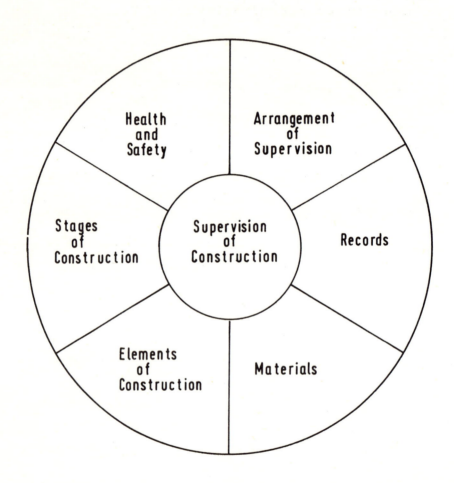

Diagram 10

10 General Observations

An alternative title for this final chapter could be 'Summing-Up and General Observations' because the chapter comprises a summary of the contents and themes of the proceeding chapters, an explanation of the diagrams and, lastly, some general observations which are more appropriately included here rather than in the individual chapters.

The chapters
It is said in the Introduction that the purpose of this book is to describe what is important in site supervision and how best to set about it; supervision requiring, among other things, a knowledge of the principles and pattern of design and a knowledge of the order in which things are done. The chapters in this book, commencing with the Introduction, have attempted to show what is entailed in supervision from a Consultant's point of view, what to look for and why, and the importance of keeping records for the purposes of recording what was done and for recording what is to come. Summarising, each chapter:

Chapter 1   deals with the arrangement of supervision.
Chapter 2   deals with the different forms of record.
Chapter 3   discusses the materials most commonly met with in construction.
Chapter 4   considers the elements of construction of which some could just as easily have been included in the proceeding chapter and others may have been better termed 'structural elements'. Nevertheless for convenience both these groups have been placed under this chapter.
Chapter 5   considers the stages passed through during the construction of a project.

These first five chapters may be described as 'general' chapters dealing with matters common to most construction projects.
Then follows two chapters dealing with particular subjects:

Chapter 6   Structural steelwork, and
Chapter 7   Earthworks

The choice of these two subjects in particular was made because each is widely encountered in a greater or lesser degree in most projects and because their technologies are in sharp contrast one with the other; the assembly of shop prefabricated units in the former, the direct winning and placing of naturally occuring materials in the latter. (The subject of reinforced concrete, rather than having a separate chapter devoted to it, has been covered in more general terms in the various chapters.)

Chapter 8   describes the important items to consider in the supervision of a selection of specialist subjects.

Chapter 9   covers the subjects of health and safety, matters very relevant to all sites.

Lastly this chapter which summarises the preceeding chapters and concludes with some general observations.

Such then is the arrangement and subject of the chapters, now some words about the diagrams.

The diagrams

At the beginning of each chapter is a diagram which presents the contents and divisions of that chapter. The diagrams have been arranged in a way which is intended to emphasise the theme followed in the writing of the chapter, the supervisory approach required, and an overall picture of the subject in question.

Diagram A   *Introduction:* shows supervision in its function as linking design and construction

Diagram 1   *Arrangement of supervision:* is in three parts and indicates (i) a simple layout of a resident engineer's or a resident architect's supervisory organisation and staffing, (ii) typical items and arrangements necessary to effect supervision of the standards of construction and the quality of materials, (iii) how inspection of certain items is effected from the design office.

Diagram 2   *Records:* shows the different types of records and their use in reports and forecasting.

Diagram 3   *Materials:* illustrates how the quality of construction materials is controlled by means of specification, inspection and sampling, and testing.

Diagram 4   *Elements of construction:* shows the importance of recognising the principles of design and the pattern of construction when supervising construction and how these are linked between the structural elements and their assembly to form the finished works.

Diagram 5   *Stages of construction:* defines five stages in the progress of a project and lists the characteristic activities of each stage from possession of site to maintenance.

Diagram 6   *Structural steelwork:* indicates the sequence followed in steelwork construction from arrival of the steel on site, through erection to final painting, and the items requiring control in each phase.

Diagram 7   *Earthworks:* indicates how control is effected and shared, through the field section and the laboratory from borrow pit to testing of the placed material, and the importance of topographical and material surveys.

Diagram 8   *Specialist construction:* explains that underlying the specialist techniques, whether land, sea or air based, are conventional principles, materials and structural elements.

Diagram 9   *Health and safety:* shows how these two matters may be considered in terms of the health and safety of the individual and the safety of the works.

Diagram 10   *General observations:* considers the whole of supervision of construction as being formed of the parts Arrangements of supervision, Records, Materials, Elements of construction, Stages of construction, and Health and safety. The parts are inter-related and should be considered severally and jointly when an activity is being supervised.

General observations

Inspection is a positive exercise and the attitude of Inspectors should be that prevention is better than cure. If things are being done incorrectly do something positive to have them corrected, don't just write about the malpractice in a daily report.

Do not expect the Contractor to take kindly to an instruction to remove several days faulty work if he has not had fair, unequivocal and repeated warnings or instructions beforehand. (He won't take kindly to it anyway so see the above remarks about positive inspection.)

As a general rule, avoid doing the Contractor's work for him even if it is difficult to stand by and see things being done 'wrongly'. Give advice by all means but avoid giving positive instructions on how a piece of work should be done; the temptations to do this are especially numerous where building crafts and trades are concerned.

Remember that the Contractor has undertaken to produce work to the standards required by the specification and that as long as these standards are being met the Contractor is reasonably free to chose his own methods for so doing.

Be wary about taking things for granted. Do not assume that others know how to do things correctly just because one knows, from experience, the correct method. When considering a new activity be prepared to start from first principles each time. In fact it is wise to do so because there is usually someone who is encountering the activity for the first time.

Because something has been done the same way for many years it doesn't necessarily mean that it has been done correctly or that methods cannot be improved. This applies to conventional as well as to 'specialised' techniques.

When a new activity starts, supervision is usually keen. Ensure that it remains keen and that attitudes do not become complacent with repetition.

Check that the Contractor's organisation is arranged adequately for each job in hand.

The attitude of 'at the Contractor's own risk' is not a very positive one and easy to condemn in principle but less easy to avoid in practice.

Think twice before instructing the removal of defective work, its replacement may cause more problems than it solves. Consider alternative means of bringing the defective work up to a satisfactory standard. Often it is better for the Contractor to carry on working and carry out remedial work later.

During site inspections, be suspicious, ferret around, make notes — don't rely on memory, vary the route, variety leads to better, more alert inspection.

One will have to observe and learn from others in many cases. However, do not hesitate to speak out if one thinks things are wrong. It is better, for example, to hold up a concrete pour, or an earthworks team for half an hour while seeking advice/decision/ guidance from a senior, than trying to sort out mistakes when there are another two or three stories on the building or another ten metres fill on an embankment. If one is proved to be wrong do not be disconcerted, it is all in the process of learning. At the same time do not be put off making a firm stand again on something one thinks or knows is wrong.

With the proviso always that their respective authorities and responsibilities should never be compromised, the Contractor/ Consultant relationship on a project should be approached as being a joint venture, as it were, to ensure the production of work which will satisfy the Client's requirements.

Recommended References

There are many good reference books, indeed the problem is often one of selecting the best book from the several available alternatives. Each publication will have its strengths and its weaknesses, and it is usually necessary to consult two or three publications before the required information has been obtained.

The excellent books listed below in chapter order cover all the subjects dealt with in this book, and many more besides. The list has been kept short deliberately to provide just a starting point for reference.

Chapter 1   Arrangement of Supervision

THE INSTITUTION OF CIVIL ENGINEERS   *Civil Engineering Procedure*   Thomas Telford, revised edition 1971, reprinted with amendments 1976

BOWYER, J T   *Small Works Supervision*   Architectural Press

Chapter 2   Records

MORONEY, M J   *Facts from Figures*   Pelican 1951, new impression 1969

Chapter 3   Materials

DIAMANT, R M E   *Applied Chemistry for Engineers*   Pitman, 3rd edition 1972

EVERETT, Alan   Mitchell's Building Series – *Materials*   Batsford new edition 1979

Chapter 4   Elements of Construction

and

Chapter 5   Stages of Construction

BLAKE, L S editor   *Civil Engineer's Reference Book*   Newnes-Butterworth, 3rd edition 1975

MERRITT, F S editor   *Standard Handbook for Civil Engineers*   McGraw-Hill 1968

FOSTER, Jack Stroud   *Structure and Fabric Part 1*   Batsford, new edition 1979

FOSTER, Jack Stroud and HARINGTON, Raymond   *Structure and Fabric Part 2*   Batsford, new edition 1978

MURDOCK, L J and BLACKLEDGE, G F *Concrete Materials and Practice*   Edward Arnold, 4th revised edition 1968

Chapter 6 **Structural Steelwork**

Steel Designers' Manual Crosby   Lockwood, 4th edition 1972

Chapter 7 **Earthworks**

Earth Manual   United States Department of the Interior, Bureau of
   Reclamation, 2nd edition 1974

Chapter 8 **Specialist Construction**

As for 4 and 5. Also:

PUGSLEY, A   *Safety of Structures*   Edward Arnold 1966

Chapter 9 **Health and Safety**

Health and Safety at Work Series booklets
Final Report of the Advisory Committee on Falsework (Bragg
   Report) from Health and Safety Executive, Forms and
   Publications, HMSO 1975

General

British Standards
Detailed specifications, these have not been listed here because of
the large number published. The specification for any project should
however list those British Standards particularly relevant to that
project.

Codes of Practice
These are usually more general in nature than British Standards
and each Code contains a mine of information on recommended
practices and procedures for the subjects in question. Those in the
Building and Civil Engineering Series are appropriate. The relevar
Codes should be listed in the project specification.

   All British Standards and Codes of Practice are listed in the
British Standards Yearbook published by the British Standards
Institution, and are available from the Sales Department, 101
Pentonville Road, London N1 9ND.

Index